MISLEADERS
WE ARE NOT LIVING IN THE LAST DAYS!
MATHEW 24

BY:

GARRETT PARRISH

DaveWarren

My brother Dave's van in Front Street in Lahaina, Maui.

DEDICATION

To those who will influence our future by overcoming the evil report of futurism (Numbers 13). To their freedom found in knowing the truth of scripture (John 5:39, 8:32, Mt.22:29), and the heart, mind and plan of God, which thing is fought hard against by the Pharisees who think they know the scriptures but forbid the honest questioning and challenging of their golden calves. To my six children and my brother Dave, who made it known from his van to visitors worldwide in Lahaina, Maui, "We are NOT living in the last days", and a special thank you to my partner and primary mentor on these matters, Terry Kashian, as well as Gary DeMar and Don Preston for drafting such revolutionary books!

Table of Contents

INTRODUCTION

For those with circumcised hearts and ears to hear (Acts 7:51), know that this book's message is to reveal the heart, mind, and plan of God in His word, which is to take dominion over the nations through the Good News of the kingdom's Great Commission, a message that has been lost in our day through the evil report of futurism (Numbers 13, Matthew 28:18-20, Revelation 2:26,27). This is my journey in understanding these things, which I break down by going verse by verse through Matthew 24, with a great emphasis on verse 14, the kingdom mandate. After reading this book, you will see that the ball is in our court, as His authority has been offered to us to shepherd and rule the nations with a staff of iron, according to Revelation 2:26,27! Futurism is the kink in the hose, which is preventing this, meaning that the kink is on our end! Do know that I've attempted to civilly reason, entreat, question and challenge many of those on the cover of this book for about two decades concerning these matters with no response. Perhaps this book will open the door for some of that. I do follow some of the advice here that I received from John Wimber at the Vineyard, which was, "Find out who you're supposed to offend and go offend them"!

CHAPTER 1

SCRIPTURE ALONE!

Jesus is the Word of Truth (John 1:1,14) Himself! The Word alone must be trusted as we follow the Reformation's battle cry, "Sola Scriptura" (Only scripture)! Scripture alone is the final authority, and every man must be considered a liar (Romans 3:4).

Whatever happened to, "I dare NOT trust the sweetest frame, but only lean on Jesus' name"?

And did not Jesus, the apostles, the reformers, going back, the prophets and Moses use the word to rebuke and correct leaders?

2 Corinthians 3:16 "All Scripture is inspired by God and beneficial for teaching, FOR REBUKE, FOR CORRECTION, for training in righteousness;"

And where is the accountability of false predictions amongst the most influential leaders in the body of Christ? Chuck Smith and Hal Lindsay both predicted a rapture in the 80's. Lindsay simply edited such out of the new editions of his book, "The Late Great Planet Earth".

Christianity Today had brought up the point of accountability prior to Lindsey's prediction date of 1988 in 1977.

They asked him what would happen if Jesus didn't return by 1988 as he had predicted, Hal Lindsey responded, "There's just a split second's difference between a hero and a bum. If I'm wrong about this, I guess I'll become a bum".

Lindsey did not become a bum but continued to sell millions of books.

Lester Sumrall did a broadcast where he walked from one station to the next, with the future year written on it, which would say something like, "1985, the rapture of the church has taken place..., 1990, the tribulation is taking place, the Antichrist is reigning..., 1992, the Millennium has begun... ". No one ever called this out! Sumrall was the same guy that was sent to Hollywood from the Midwest in the 1940's, I believe, to see about reaching it for Christ. He returned with the evil report (Numbers 13) , that it was unredeemable. The church handed it over to the evil one!

John Hagee made specific predictions to occur during blood moons in 2014 and 2015. None of them came to pass! Jonathan Cahn made similar predictions to occur during the Jewish Smitah year around the same time. The book was called "Mystery of the Smitah". It would have been more edifying, at least to our bodies, if it had been a book about the "Mystery of the Fajita", because the Smitah hit the fan as nothing of what he predicted occurred, but he moved on to his next book! We have some sick Christians as a result of all these false predictions!

Proverbs 13:12 *"Hope deferred makes the heart sick."*

"Mystery of the Fajita"

For the world looking at these multitudes of false predictions, which they assured us was Bible Prophecy, the conclusion is that the Bible must not be true, or at best it's not clear at all, it's anyone's guess as to what it's saying!

In Acts 17:11, Paul did not argue concerning his apostolic authority, but of the authority of scripture alone!

"These were more noble than those in Thessalonica, in that they received the word with all readiness of mind, and searched the scriptures daily, whether those things were so."

You don't hear this in pulpits today!

Proverbs 18:17 "The first to speak in court sounds right— until the cross-examination begins."

1 Kings 22 reveals that four hundred were affirming the word to be one thing on a matter, while Micaiah responded, not so!

"Unless I am convinced by Scripture and plain reason - I do not accept the authority of the popes and councils, for they have contradicted each other - my conscience is captive to the Word of God. I cannot and I will not recant anything, for to go against conscience is neither right nor safe." -Martin Luther (1521)"

The first point I'd like to make is that many of these leaders on the cover have been, and are, men of God, bringing the truth of the Good News and the word of God to many. However, they are misleading the people of God on 2/3 of the New Testament's teachings! RC Sproul found that 2/3 of the New Testament is addressing eschatology, the study of the end things.

Chuck Smith brought the word of God to me very personally when he did a message entitled, "Let's go to Rome, Paul" in 1983. It was a tailer made word for the direction of my life at the exact time I needed it (Proverbs 25:11). It was along these lines, Paul had suffered defeat in Jerusalem, he was encouraged by the Lord saying, OK Paul, now, let's go to Rome, where he would minister effectively to so many. I had just broken up with a girl, and God was saying, "let's go on to this football scholarship that's ahead for you"! Also, Chuck's format of studying the Bible from cover to cover, chapter by chapter and verse by verse was foundational for me! I would talk to Chuck and his wife Kay as a box person at Vons grocery store on 17th street in Costa Mesa. Kay later encouraged me when I was making a commitment to teach the word only, as I was leaving my football career in 1987. I also highly respect Jack Hibbs for making stances against the Commie California politicians in our day! However, those evil political leaders are there, because as I will point out, the evil report of dispensationalism (Numbers 13) has invited them in! Talk about shooting yourself in the foot! Lance Walnau has some very powerful truths of a kingdom word to influence our culture, as does Joseph Z. Yet, all these men of God are functioning in the faulty framework of dispensationalism, which is shooting the body of Christ in the feet, instead of putting Satan under them (Romans 16:20).

Here is The Evil Report of the Giants verses the Giant Grapes, fruit of the Spirit to possess the land.

Numbers 13:24-33

"The place was called the brook Eshcol, because of THE CLUSTER OF GRAPES which the children of Israel cut down from thence. And they returned from searching of the land after forty days. And they went and came to Moses, and to Aaron, and to all the congregation of the children of Israel, unto the wilderness of Paran, to Kadesh; and brought back word unto them, and unto all the congregation, and shewed them the fruit of the land. And they told him, and said, We came unto the land whither thou sentest us, and surely it floweth with milk and honey; and this is the fruit of it. Nevertheless the people be strong that dwell in the land, and the cities are walled, and very great: and moreover we saw the children of Anak there. The Amalekites dwell in the land of the south: and the Hittites, and the Jebusites, and the Amorites, dwell in the mountains: and the Canaanites dwell by the sea, and by the coast of Jordan. And Caleb stilled the people before Moses, and said, LET US GO UP AT ONCE AND POSSESS IT; FOR WE ARE WELL ABLE TO OVERCOME IT. But the men that went up with him said, WE BE NOT ABLE to go up against the people; for they are stronger than we. And they brought up AN EVIL REPORT of the land which they had searched unto the children of Israel, saying, The land, through which we have gone to search it, is a land that eateth up the inhabitants thereof; and all the people that we saw in it are men of a great stature. And there we saw THE GIANTS, the sons of Anak, which come of the giants: and WE WERE IN OUR OWN SIGHT AS GRASSHOPPERS, and so we were in their sight."

CHAPTER 2

MY STORY OF COMING TO FAITH

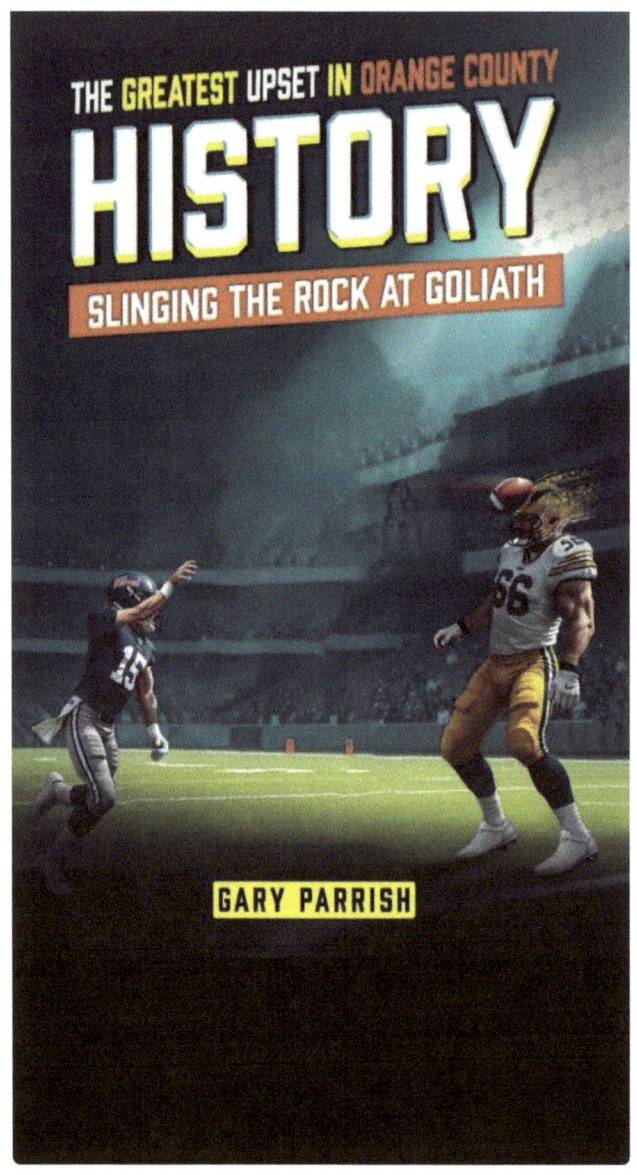

I came to faith through reading "The Living Bible, Self Help Edition" in 1979. It was a Sunday night and I could feel the looming pressure mounting as we'd begin practicing football the next day for Edison High! I played quarterback at Newport Harbor and we'd never lost to Edison and had won the Sunset League the year prior as sophomores. This Included beating Edison, Mater Dei, Servite, Long Beach Millikan, and tying Fountain Valley. As I look back at my High School's history, I can see the hand of God at work as it was the launching pad for the

Jesus Movement, where Lonnie Frisbee began preaching on our campus. It was here that Greg Laurie came to faith in hearing Lonnie preach. Newport Beach was also the home of John Wayne and was the birthplace of the Reagan Revolution, which began with a group of Newport businessmen, my classmates parents. It was later the home of Kobe Bryant, who's Mamba Mentality fit right in with the culture.

Our senior year (1980), Edison and Fountain Valley in our league would be officially ranked number one and two in the nation! And this '79 Edison team was far better than the '80 team , which the LA Times acknowledged about 20 years later. Perhaps it was this pressure that moved me to consider any kind of outside help I could get? What was there to lose in looking into this Jesus guy, I thought. All I knew about Him was the pictures I'd seen during Easter of Him on a cross.

I had been out carousing one summer night in '79 and two of my friends were talking to a guy and arguing with him as I came around the corner by the Pavilion at the Fun Zone in Balboa. The guy began to plead with my friends, almost to the point of tears, sincerely but boldly proclaiming, "Without Jesus Christ in your life, you WILL go to hell!" As I began to consider this Jesus Christ guy, I realized that the consequences of Him not in my life could be catastrophic! I had suffered a lot of injuries, like broken bones, sprained ankles, etc. and had felt excruciating pain before, so I knew that I surely didn't want to suffer hell someday! I had no idea how God could show me if this Jesus Christ guy was needed in my life somehow? But I did believe that God was the creator out there somewhere, as I remembered seeing pictures of the sun and the size of the flames coming out from it being much bigger than the earth, etc., so I prayed, "I know you're out there somewhere, so however you could possibly show me, I don't know how, but I'm giving myself to honestly look into this matter".

I figured that if nothing happens, and I didn't expect that anything would, I will at least know in my conscience that I had considered this Jesus Christ guy being in my life and would conclude that it all wasn't anything more real than some old fish story. I thought that I'd just continue the path that I was on. I was quite content and happy being on my way to playing QB in college and believed I could work hard enough to improve enough and make it to the NFL, while I was partying it up along the way!

I dusted off the "Living Bible" that my mom had gotten me. She had heard that I was going to Saint Andrews Presbyterian Youth Group on Sundays, so she'd gotten me "The Living Bible, Self Help Edition". I was only going there, because I was usually partying on Saturday nights with my friend, Tony Shepardson, and would stay the night at his house on Lido Island. His grandmother would make me the offer of a free brunch, if I came to church first! I began to read the intro which recommended starting in the book of Mark, as it was relatively short and to the point in revealing the life of Jesus.

As I began to read, I was amazed at how simple and clear it was to understand! I was told by my mom that the bible was "Hard to understand, like reading Greek". As I began reading through the chapters I began to be curious as to what Jesus was going to do next. He would outwit his opponents and perform miracles, etc., and I began to actually enjoy reading this bible. This was really something because I had always hated to read! This bible also had other verses for various issues that we all face, such as being,

DISCOURAGED: "Be strong! Be courageous! Do not be afraid of them! For the Lord your God will be with you. He will neither fail you nor forsake you" (Deut. 31:6).

FEARFUL: "Fear not, for I am with you. Do not be dismayed. I am your God. I will strengthen you; I will help you; I will uphold you with my victorious right hand" (Isaiah 41:10).

INSECURE: "If God is on our side, who can ever be against us" (Romans 8:28)? This was shocking to me as I read it, as I'd always thought that God had quite a few things against me. There was more good news here, "I am holding you by your right hand-I, the Lord your God-and I say to you, Don't be afraid; I am here to help you" (Isaiah 41:13). "Don't be afraid, for I am with you. Don't be discouraged, for I am your God. I will strengthen you and help you. I will hold you up with my victorious right hand" (Isaiah 41:10). That is why we can say without any doubt or fear, "The Lord is my Helper, and I am not afraid of anything that mere man can do to me" (Hebrews 13:6). And I figured that I needed to deal with the following matter, as it seemed to be part of the package deal with all of this good news!

GUILTY: "Come, let's talk this over! Says the Lord; no matter how deep the stain of your sins, I can take it out and make you as clean as freshly fallen snow. Even if you are stained as red as crimson, I can make you white as wool" (Isaiah 1:18)!

As I continued to read through the book of Mark, I knew in my "knower", that Jesus was in fact true! As I read each night that week, I would experience this euphoria of peace, comfort, and happiness! It was unlike anything I had ever experienced before! It was better than the euphoria I had when I would get drunk off beer, which was something I thought was the ultimate that life had to offer! Yet, there was no hangover with this!

As I read through the book of Mark that week, I came across this verse in Mark 11:23,24, "Jesus said to the disciples, "If you have faith in God-this is the absolute truth-you can say to this Mount of Olives, "Rise up and fall into the Mediterranean," and your command will be obeyed. All that's required is that you really believe and have no doubt. Listen to me! You can pray for anything, and if you believe, you have it; its yours"! As this stuff was all new to me, I concluded that either these words of Jesus were true, or they were not! So, I would pray them, along with all the other encouraging and exhilarating verses, and I would pray that we would beat the number one team in the land, Edison! We did, 17-13, and the full story is in my book, "The Greatest Upset in Orange County History, Slinging The Rock at Goliath". I got in with seven minutes left and scored two touchdowns and set up a field goal to defeat an NFL quarterback, tight end and a running back that USC prioritized above Hershel Walker, whom John Robinson said would be his tailback as he kept Marcus Allen at fullback. Kerwin Bell went to the Rams camp to test before his senior year at Edison, as Edison's Middle Linebacker, Bill Malavasi was the son of Rams head coach Ray Malavasi. Kerwin ran a faster 40 time than all of the Rams players!

I believe that God created me to overcome insurmountable odds and win! I believe that the Bible reveals this to be in His nature and plan, which I believe has been distorted and perverted to create week and non influential Christians!

On my journey in the faith my life was turned upside down and transformed a few years later in 1982, I had literally been told that I was the next Roger Staubach after my Junior year, being recruited as a quarterback by BYU, UCLA, and Arizona. A shoulder injury, after throwing 700 passes a day, ended my career as a quarterback. I graduated and worked at Vons grocery store, and went from rehearsing Heisman Trophy speeches and pondering if it would be possible to go straight to the NFL or not from High School, to being scolded about price checks as a box person. At this time I met up with a sold out Jesus Freak guy named Paul Broggie. He used to do a Bible Study with Lonnie Frisbee. Due see "The Jesus Revolution" with Kelsey Grammer to learn about

Lonnie. We met house to house (Acts 20:20) with a small group of us and Paul exemplified a life fully given to Jesus in every aspect! At one of the first meetings, I remember his girlfriend Amanda playing the Guitar, and she and Paul were really singing, sort of a bit annoying and intimidating to me. I mean singing with an Acoustic guitar just seemed a little "gay" and weak to me anyway, but I humbled myself and thought I'd at least give it a try. As I stepped out and began to sing, Paul and Amanda were very gentle and welcoming me to the party as they softly said, "Praise the Lord". During the meetings, Paul would begin to talk about his day with real testimonies of how he was living by faith in his commitment and dealing in prayer and faith in his daily interactions and decisions! He really interpreted everything through this lens of faith without any complaining, but in humility and by giving thanks and praise, all through a life of prayer! We would follow his example and begin to give thanks for this and that and begin declarations of thankfulness and commitment of everything we did, and Who we were doing it for throughout the day.

I would begin to have this joy and filling of the Spirit that Paul would explain was God giving us His Spirit without measure, overflowing out of our being! Paul exhorted me to ask for a prayer language, to speak in tongues. At first you think it's silly, just you, but then the Holy Spirit takes over and begins to pray for various things that you don't even know that you need prayer for, was my experience. My life was being transformed in these meetings. Some Friday nights we'd stay as late as 2:00 AM! One Friday night, after the meeting ending at 2:00 am at Tony's house on Lido Island, I got in my grandmother's '64 Ford Falcon and had a deep prayer that came up in my heart after so much hurt from my football career. I had always wanted to play at USC.

I prayed, "Lord, I, honestly, would rather have this (the joy, peace, comfort, and completeness found in the Holy Spirit) which I'm experiencing right now than score a touchdown for USC"! I realized also that if I had gone on successfully as a QB to USC, I would never have gotten to the point of humbling myself and having this experience! My Newport mentality wouldn't have even allowed me to hang out with people that weren't up to the Newport Beach dress standards.

I began to watch TBN and hear the testimonies of God being real in people's lives like Jan and Paul Crouch and their guests. I was being exhorted to never complain, be bitter, or murmur! I would only give praise and thanks for all circumstances! I would pray through the night being filled with joy and thoughts that I'd write down, because I was being overwhelmed and knew that I couldn't remember all of the new thoughts, feelings, and wisdom that I was receiving. I'd get up from my sleep to go to the bathroom and be so filled with joy, it truly was unspeakable.

This was all being ingrained into me by the Spirit! I remember being touched so deeply by God's overwhelming love that I had to ask the Lord to stop, it was too much! Other times, I remember being so deep in experiencing His presence, love, joy, and peace, that I didn't even know if I was in my body or not! I would listen to Keith Green's music and remember one day hearing it and just breaking down with tears of surrender! I remember hearing the lyrics, "I tried to see your plan for me, but I only acted like I knew"! The joy, peace, patience, kindness, and comfort through the presence of the Lord, was beyond comprehension! I would be in a state of prayer and would be thinking of all the testimonies I'd heard on TBN, and my life was being turned upside down! I even prayed to the Lord, that if I got back into another sexual relationship before marriage, that I'm asking that you literally take me home, physically kill me!

I remember working at Vons one day and as was my custom, I would wait for the opportune time to look over at my fellow grocery bagger, and lust at her in her tight white pants. As my habit was to do this, for the first time, this thought came to me instead that that would not be a loving thing to do so toward this girl! I literally stepped back and said, "This is not me having thoughts like this"! It was just about my first pure thought! There was someone else giving me these thoughts! I was being revolutionized! There was another checker that worked there, which most of the box persons thought was quite contentious, to put it nicely! I began to try out being friendly and responding with a soft answer and humble myself in response to her, and my relationship with her changed! It became very positive, peaceful, and even friendly!

At one of those home meetings, I remember seeing a book on the desk at my friend Tony Shepardson's house entitled, "What the World is Coming To", as the cover had a picture of the globe with a stick of dynamite stuck through it, and the fuse was nearly burnt to the end. It was by Chuck Smith. After experiencing such reality of Jesus in my life, I saw this book and asked Paul, "This is crazy stuff, right"? He said no, it's the Bible, it's good. I set this on a shelf in my mind. Shortly thereafter, I began to read that book on my beach chair in front of my grandmother's house on Orange Avenue in Costa Mesa. I remember it like it was yesterday. I would pray and ask the Lord to speak to me, and as I began to read, I really liked what Chuck Smith was saying at the beginning. He had such an easiness about him, not adamant, saying that there are different interpretations, preterist, etc... Later editions removed this part. As the leader of the Jesus movement, he talked about man looking at the outward appearance and God looking at the heart (1 Samuel 16:7). And that the hippies were looking beyond materialism and into the deeper matters of spiritual things. I asked the Lord if I should, not if I could, join up with them, as Calvary Chapel was located right here in my backyard? The clear answer was, "No, that I want to teach you and mature you in learning of me". Again, not that I couldn't do this, so I asked if I could join up with some of the things going on there, as it was a real movement. I was also thinking that things would also be easier by grabbing on to the coat tails of this movement, than getting my own source from Him personally, which was, honestly, much more difficult. Paul had deeply instilled in me that the Holy Spirit was my teacher and that "you have no need for any man to teach you" (1 John 2:27). The Holy Spirit would make it clear that that meant Paul as well, which of course, is what he too believed. I reasoned with God about how I would still maintain what I had with him but would just get some ease with the flow of this movement, etc..

I met with Calvary Costa Mesa for 5 years, '82- '87 and did really benefit from some things learned from Randy Ziegler who was the most anointed evangelist, by a hundred times, that I have ever heard! Randy had me meet with him in his office, his station wagon haha, and said he wanted me to lead a home group and to put him out of a job. I said I'd get back to him and deferred such as I was consumed with football and school. Randy preached after the Saturday night concerts and led the Tuesday night "Surf Fellowship Bible Study". Again, it was the most real evangelism as it was prophetic in touching hearts (1 Corinthians 14:25). Randy truly had a kingdom dominion mindset.

Randy Zeigler. Never have I heard anything close to the anointing I witnessed in Randy to evangelize.

Chuck Smith was great at going through the Bible verse by verse and pointing to the New Testament when reading through the old and seeing its fulfillment in Jesus.

CHAPTER 3

KINGDOM NOW, DOMINION CHALLENGE!

At this time a close friend was on staff as a pastor, and he would just rail on the Vineyard Movement as being demonic and adventuring into the gifts of the Spirit and leaving the word of God. He was parodying things he'd heard in the pastor's meetings he was having with Chuck Smith. I knew that these were half truths, full lies, that I was hearing, because I knew the fullness of the work of the Spirit. All the charismatic ministries such as TBN, "Eagles Nest", etc were way off. It was only they who were "balanced" and could and should be trusted. I knew that the half truth that they proclaimed concerning the importance of the scriptures, true, but the practice of the gifts was demonic, was a whole lie. This guy would mock and degrade people after they'd come in his office for counseling, after ACTING so sincere with the people. I new that Paul was now meeting with the Vineyard in Yorba Linda with John Wimber, whom the Calvary guys were saying was a false prophet and teacher! Paul would give me new perspectives on seeing the work of the Spirit, backed by scripture. I had been taught to reject such work, thinking that scripture supported this idea. God was calling me to make a choice as I was also to make a choice concerning to continue and pursue an NFL career after many injuries, or to leave it and pursue the ministry of the word in some capacity? As I got prayer about going back to Tucson, the prayers were as such, "Lord, he believes he should go, bless him", I.e.. We don't think he's hearing you…. I said in my heart, "OK, I'm not going, because I'm not hearing what I believe you're saying in my heart to do. As they finished and my eyes were still closed, this guy came over out of nowhere and started prophesying over me, something I'd never experienced. He said, "I've called you, don't look back, don't even try to understand, it's not by might, or power but by my Spirit says the Lord"! Bam, the secrets of my heart were made known (1 Corinthians 14:25)! This guy had just come out of a "Believers Meeting" on Wednesday nights at Calvary Costa Mesa!

So, I stepped out and chose the word and went back to Tucson with $10 in my pocket that my dad had given me with no more years left on my scholarship. I had been talking with the Rams Tight End coach, Norv Turner and called to let him know of my decision. I was also in a great dilemma with wanting to marry a girl from the U of A that I had dated. I was needing all that God had, so I went to The Vineyard Christian Fellowship in Tucson. This is because I had heard some good testimonies of being ministered to through the gift of prophecy at the Vineyard, through Paul.

From my first time meeting there, I had established that I wasn't going to go for any fake, kind of, maybe stuff, only what was real! I would hear these detailed prophecies given after worship songs that caused me to say in my heart, "There's a voice that I know", that is, "His Voice", I didn't have time to give to something that was some kind of guess work! I was laying my life down here! Helen Hawks would prophesy only things that were the secrets of my heart, that no one else knew! (1 Corinthians 14:25). I was ready and willing to call out anything that wasn't true! When she'd say, "You said to me in prayer…", that was exactly what I'd said, verbatim! Again, if it wasn't true, I was ready to jump on that and loudly say, "I didn't say this or that in prayer"! It seemed like Helen prophesied to the T over me a hundred times! She prophesied over me one time about being influenced by a wolf that taught me to bite and devour, by speaking against and not receiving those who are in the body. Much of this was taught to me under the guise of "discernment", which was to reject anyone and everyone that was not Calvary Chapel! I thought, who has spoken such things into my life? Was it Chuck Smith who'd had great influence in my life, the Lord said, no, you've heard my voice through him. Was it Paul? No. you've heard my voice through him. Is it Greg (Not Greg Laurie), bingo, as clear as day is how the Holy Spirit answered me! In prayer meetings Helen would challenge me with what the Vineyard was teaching about "Kingdom Now" (Dominion) stuff, and it was a real struggle as I'd been taught that this is false, and it's all about a kingdom in Israel some day, after "Bible Prophecy" was fulfilled and we are raptured out of here.

As I was challenged on these things, I would just begin to think of the concepts I was taught and before I could even say them, my words would fall to the floor! I had even changed my major to Political Science, because I was going to find out who the Antichrist in Europe was!

Helen with Gavin MacLeod.

Helen on the mission field.

Helen with friends.

One day in the spring of 1988, my roommate at the University of Arizona, Keith Moody was praying, after turning down an offer by the Dallas Cowboys to become a free agent. Keith was 6'5 260 and ran a 4.6 forty. He played Defensive Line. His neck and back injuries were so severe, that he realized that his body just couldn't continue. He prayed that day, "Lord, well, at least I'm tall". That night I brought him to a Vineyard home group and Helen prophesied over him and said, "You walk tall with man and you walk tall with me"! God was just encouraging him that He hears Keith's prayers and for him to continue to walk and talk in communion with Him.

A certain prophet (sorry my cessationist friends, not sorry) named CL (Clearance) Moore from Kansas would come through the Vineyard once in a while. My friend sitting next to me, Michelle, was told by Helen over and over again that God was giving her boldness. CL Moore walked down the isle and spoke to her and said, "God is giving you boldness"! CL Moore really challenged me by saying that "God's kingdom is not about some sand over in the Middle East, but it's here right now!" I was taught at Calvary Chapel that all this "Kingdom Now" stuff was false teaching. I was so challenged, that I had to give this "new teaching", new to my ears, a look at in scripture. I looked up verses like, "You HAVE come to the heavenly Jerusalem", not that you will someday (Hebrews 12:22).

Then I read how that believers are to identify with this "Jerusalem, which is above", and not the Old Covenant capitol city of Jerusalem (Galatians 4:25,26,). And then how the Holy Spirit refers to New Covenant people as "The Israel of God" (Galatians 6:16). I later learned that Old Covenant Israel was a type of Jesus, the ultimate promised land and dwelling place of God. "Out of Egypt have I called my son" (Hosea 11:1), Israel the Old Covenant type, and "Out of Egypt have I called my Son", Jesus the New Covenant reality of what that type was pointing to. Jesus hasn't replaced Israel, He IS Israel! The sign wasn't the real thing, it was only pointing to the real thing, the reality, Jesus!

CHAPTER 4

THE FINGER OF GOD WRITING ON MY HEART, NOT ANOTHER!

Fast forward to living on Maui, where I raised my six children. We were attending King's Cathedral where the common "understanding" of end times was Hal Lindsey (Late Great Planet Earth) premillennial dispensational teaching, which crept in here and there. I began reverting to such concepts and said something about this and my wife Audrey said, "That already happened". I thought, boy, she really believes that in saying it without batting an eye! I thought that I needed to get to the bottom of the matter. So, I set out to read through the book of Revelation and read it as though I never had. It was the first book I studied; it should have been the last.

Calvary Chapel offered a 2 for1 package deal, accept Jesus and it's the end times as the Antichrist is setting up in Europe, Russia is going to attack Israel, and we are all about to do a disappearing act and the planet will then get nuked! Again, the first book I read to study the Bible with was called, "What the World is Coming To", by Chuck Smith. It had a picture on the cover of a stick of dynamite in the globe with the fuse lit. This was a commentary on the book of

Revelation. Let me emphasize again, it was the first book of the Bible I'd studied, when it should have been the last! I had been indoctrinated by such books and teachings on the subject. In reading the book of Revelation, I realized that if I could know who "the unfaithful harlot" was, I could understand the book! The revelation came to me, in order to be unfaithful this character had to have been in a marriage relationship before!

Who had been in a marriage covenant with God before? It was Old Covenant Israel, who is even called this exact thing in Isaiah 1:21, "How is the faithful city become a harlot"! The harlot is in Revelation 17:5. Boom, game, set, match! Furthermore, "The Great City is Babylon, mentioned about a dozen times in Revelation and "The Great City" is identified as "the city where our Lord was crucified" (Rev.11:8). Where was our Lord crucified? "It cannot be that a prophet would perish outside of Jerusalem" (Luke 13:33). Very simple, Jerusalem is the Great City, Babylon, which is being judged throughout the book of Revelation! One more helper here is that the word "world" or "earth" throughout the book's judgments is never once referring to the globe (Kosmos) but is always referring to the "land" ("Ge" as in geography), which Young's Translation gets right. It is often times the word "Oikoumene" that is used, meaning the inhabited Roman world, not the globe (Luke 2:1). I read a book that my friend Mike Day had given me by Gary Demar called, "Last Days Madness".

This book utterly turned my world upside down in affirming this truth! So, I was becoming fruitful in my understanding of scripture. Helen had prophesied over me that God was going to write on my heart with His finger (Hebrews 8:10), that it would not be written upon with the finger of another, which is what had happened at my time at Calvary Costa Mesa. This subject of the last things, eschatology, makes up 2/3 of the entire New Testament, according to R.C. Sproul. It is so freeing to know the truth, that the last days WERE the last days of the Old Covenant age (Matthew 24:3, 34, Hebrews 1:2, 9:26) and that there is no pre-determined worldwide destruction, according to bible prophecy in our day!

I shared some of these things with my friend Earl Thurner. I had coached his son Jed in football. Jed later started 1 Nation 1 Day, a powerful missionary ministry. Jed later told me that I changed his life. I had taught him receiver skills well, as he burned Shane Victorino (Boston Red Socks), the fastest guy in the state, on a 9 route. I encouraged him in commitment when he said that he wanted to play linebacker or safety in college. I told him that if it was a linebacker, he needed to

21

get his sleeping bag and pillow and move into the weight room, that the bench was his new bed. He was already swift of foot from the double tires I'd trained him and his teammates on. If he wanted to play safety in college, then his new home was on the track where he was never to leave. I believe he was All American at Azusa Pacific and nearly played in the NFL as an Outside Linebacker.

Earl wasn't quite sure about what I was believing. He then asked to meet up and we talked for about an hour in a half on a drive over to Embassy Suites, to pick up a check and back. He told me after our talk that he wanted to talk to me because he was concerned for me, that I was being deceived in what I believed. After the talk he said that he was no longer concerned. In fact, he started prophesying over me and said that I needed to start a radio show on this subject and have callers with questions and to answer them as I had with him. He had given me a word a number of years earlier that I would have an uncanny word about the kingdom that people would say, "I haven't heard that before", and that I would go from place-to-place sharing, that it wouldn't be for just one place.

I was hesitant to step out and do this, but after a year I reached out to the local talk radio station KKOI 1110am, which had Rush Limbaugh and other political shows on it. Our friend Wibitz Stewart had a show on here as well, "Girl's Just Want to Have Fun". The manager said yes, and the rest was prophecy in our history! The name of the broadcast was "Bible Prophecy Fulfilled". Most of the questions were so sincere.

A lot of new age thinkers, agnostics/atheists, and even Muslims would call and say how that they really liked the show! We would emphasize free speech and let them fully express their thoughts. This is because I had called into "To Every Man an Answer" (Calvary Satellite Network), and very civilly questioned Hal Lindsey on the air, and they hung up on me! Terry Kashian and Mike Day would join me regularly as we went through the entire book of Revelation and other prophetic passages like Matthew 24. After 2 years I was able to get us on to the Christian Station in Honolulu, KGU-Salem Radio. They had a nice studio where I'd go every Saturday morning at 11 am.

They also had an Oldies station where I was able to talk to and learn a lot from a guy named Tom Moffatt. Tom was the promoter that brought Elvis to Hawaii as well as many other great performers like the Rolling Stones, Jimmy Hendrix, Elton John, Frank Sinatra, and Bruno Mars who started out on Oahu. The show was syndicated, being aired in about 9 other cities around the country, including Phoenix, Tucson, Albuquerque, and throughout the Southeast as well as Scranton, Pennsylvania where Joe Biden and the Dunder Mifflin people listened regularly! I was really seeing fruitfulness in the ministry of the word! (www.Bible ProphecyFulfilled.net)

CHAPTER 5

GOD'S DIRECTORY

The Word of Truth wrongly divided? Dismantling the Dispensational Delusion.

Leaders need to know where they are in order to lead others in the right direction. If leaders don't, indeed, know where they are, how can they then properly lead others? Again, eschatology, the study of the end things, is what two thirds of the New Testament scriptures contents are talking about, according to RC Sproul. If leaders are in error concerning two thirds of the New Testament, then they are absolutely misleading teachers! If one enters a mall and looks at the directory, and it says that "YOU ARE HERE", then you have an accurate map to find your way to the desired destination. If the directory's designer is mistaken in saying that you are "HERE", when in fact you are not, but in an entirely different location, that designer is going to be responsible for misdirecting many! The followers of such a design are not going to reach their destination with any clarity, to say the least, and will most likely experience a lot of confusion, frustration, and disfunction! The designer of this directory needs to be fired, and it needs to be REPLACED, true replacement theology, with the correct diagram in order to rightly lead others on the right path to reach their destination!

The ultimate directory for Christians is the word of God. The Holy Spirit says to "rightly divide the word of truth" (2 Timothy 2:15). This is making it clear that the word of truth can be wrongly divided! The Pharisees were definitely wrongly dividing the word of truth! The reformers brought about some corrections in rightly dividing the word of truth to those who were wrongly dividing it! Every move of God brings about this correction, and those being corrected are the most resistant to it! Jesus Himself is "THE TRUTH", so we know that He wants the WORD OF TRUTH to be RIGHTLY DIVIDED, not WRONGLY DIVIDED! The first and foremost result of the truth is that it brings freedom!

John 8:32 "You shall know the truth, and the truth shall make you free.'"

The inference is clear, if you don't know the truth, you are not free, but in bondage!

I hear the charge, "You just want to be right". Um yes, RIGHTLY dividing the word of truth (2 Timothy 2:15) as, "RIGHTeousness and truth are the foundations of His throne" (Psalm 89:14)! And the kingdom of God is "RIGHTeousness, peace and joy in the Holy Spirit (Romans 14:17). Oh, we just need Jesus and love, not doctrine", I often here. Again, Jesus is THE TRUTH and His love, "rejoices in THE TRUTH" (1 Corinthians 13:7). Did not Jesus spend the majority of His ministry teaching (Doctrine) with signs and wonders performed for the purpose of confirming His doctrine? Does not teaching give us the correct thinking? Jesus's first words in preaching were, "The kingdom of God is at hand, change the way you're thinking/repent" (Mark 1:15)! Particularly, change the way your thinking concerning the kingdom of God, as the people were thinking that the kingdom was to come by observation, in the physical city of Jerusalem (Luke 17:20,21, John 4:21-24)! It must be noted that this false teaching of futurism proclaims these same misunderstandings! The kingdom of God...IS righteousness, peace and joy in the Holy Spirit" (Romans 14:17), period! Don't add to The Holy Spirit's words in the clear revelation and literal definition of what the kingdom of God is in scripture to fit your religious concepts! We've come to the New Covenant capital city, "the heavenly Jerusalem ", "the Jerusalem which is above", where all things become new (Hebrews 12:22, Galatians 4:26, 2 Corinthians 5:17/Revelation 21:5), including these types and shadows of the old covenant! Jerusalem was not a type of itself, but of

THE NEW JERUSALEM! True teaching gives us the correct thinking, to think like God thinks. We are to be renewed in our minds (Ephesians 4:23, Romans 12:2). The Vineyard was Israel, and is now Jesus, The Vine (Isaiah 5, John 15:1). The temple is now Jesus (John 2:21, 12:6, 1 Corinthians 3:16)! He is the sacrifice (John 1:29). He is the Sabbath rest (Matthew 11:29). He is the Passover (Mark 14:22-24). And yes, He is the New Covenant Nation, the only place of blessings and salvation! Israel, the old covenant type, "Out of Egypt have I called my son" (Hosea 11:1), and the New Testament reality of Jesus, "Out of Egypt have I called my Son" (Matthew 2:15). The fulfillment of the type, which cannot be a type of itself, is Jesus and Jesus alone! Dispensational teaching REPLACES Jesus with the type. Jesus said that "the kingdom shall be taken from you (Old Covenant Israel) and given to A NATION bearing fruit" (Matthew 21:43). What nation was it given to? "You are a holy NATION" (1 Peter 2:9). Those in Jesus make up this nation! The words "IN CHRIST" are used around a hundred times, maybe more, in the New Testament. It is the ultimate and only safe and blessed dwelling place of God! The charge of "Replacement Theology" comes back on dispensationalists as they are replacing Jesus with modern Israel. He's just not all that and enough for them! Jesus has fulfilled all of the Old Testament types; therefore, the Old Covenant has passed away and been REPLACED with the New Covenant! The natural man, the old man, always wants to hold onto something natural of the old man in the Old Covenant, including a natural kingdom!

Wrong teaching creates wrong thinking, leading to the wrong actions! It was, "the doctrine/teaching of the Nicolaitanes" that caused the "deeds of the Nicolaitanes" (Revelation 2:6,15). The very next word to them is to "Repent, meaning to change the way you're thinking" (Revelation 2:16)!

If we are Jesus' representatives, even His very body, "The Pillar and ground of the truth" (1Timothy 3:15), but what we are saying concerning 2/3 of His word is not true, then the consequences are to be catastrophic, and we are absolutely misrepresenting Him! This is the case, as Christian leaders and teachers have brought about the near collapse of Western Christian Civilization! The timing of this catastrophe coincides exactly with the introduction of Dispensational Teaching, promoted by John Nelson Darby in the 1830's, and propelled through the Scofield Reference Bible in the US through C.I. Scofield in 1909. It was first brought to Dallas Theological Cemetery (Not a typo), then spread to denominations and seminaries nationwide. It was the first Bible of its kind, with notes taking up much of each page instructing the reader to what Scofield believed the passage was talking about. Dispensationalism teaches that God has dispensed the time that we're living in as "the last days" of the earth, as men and culture become worse and worse, darker and darker (Consider 1st Century Roman morality) the Laodicean church age, therefore it is all about to be destroyed, before an imaginary antichrist individual takes over the world for the devil, by which time Christians do a disappearing act, the modern nation of Israel re institutes animal sacrifice, God destroys 2/3 of them, then He nukes the whole place and starts over again. Not a word of this is true but is the imagination of the carnal mind wrongly dividing the word of truth! This is truly THE EVIL REPORT of our day (Numbers 13)! If Christians rejected this nonsense, they would turn the world upside down (Acts 17:6) in two weeks!

It was in 1927 that Oswald J Smith wrote the books, "When Antichrist Reigns" and "Is the Antichrist at Hand". He said that Mussolini was the Antichrist. Others preached the same about Hitler. As a result of the church's expectation and proclamation of evil prevailing, we saw a century of bloodshed and destruction! Much more of this is explained later in this book as we break down the authority to rule offered to believers (Psalm 2/Revelation 2:26,27, Matthew 28:18-20).

The Dispensational paradigm is a strategy from the gates of hell, which allows the evil one to take over the world! Again, we just experienced the near collapse of Western Christian civilization in 2020, because of it! Do realize that the Communist left is at about 48% and those opposing it are around 49% in the Popular vote!

If the Christians in California alone, believed in long term goals and voted, the rest of the country and world would follow suit! The political slogan says, "as goes California, so goes the rest of the country and in turn, the world "! Perhaps 10 million Christians in the state do not vote! I will point out that dispensationalism of late has been exported primarily from Southern California!

Hal Lindsey (Los Angeles) sold 30 million copies of "The Late Great Planet Earth" in 1970. Around this same time, Chuck Smith formed one of the largest Denominations in the world, which propagates dispensationalism with more passion than it preaches the gospel itself! Calvary Costa Mesa was my home church, and the Jesus movement did not start this way, but dispensationalism is the primary deal breaker with this movement with a hoard of false teachings on this matter!

Again, do note that Hal Lindsey and Chuck Smith both made the prediction that Jesus was going to return in the 80's, because that was forty years after Israel had become a nation in 1948. Virtually no one has called them out and held them accountable. The outsider looking in is left with, "I guess the Bible isn't true, if it predicted such and it didn't happen", or at best, "it means whatever you want it to mean ". In the 1990's, Tim Lahaye (San Diego) began writing the "Left Behind Series". This defeatist and departure mentality has defiled the minds of Christian's! The Left Behind series has sold more copies than any other book series in history, 70 million!

One of the major tenants of this belief system is that there is to be a soon (Does "soon" mean the same thing it did in the first century, Revelation 1:1,3) pre-tribulation rapture. The belief places DANIEL'S 70th WEEK into our future, with the destruction of the city of Jerusalem and the temple (Daniel 9:24-27). They also insert an unannounced antichrist into the passage, where "Messiah the prince" is rightly Jesus Christ in 9:25, but the next verse they assign "Messiah…the prince (9:26)", the exact same words to be an un-introduced "antichrist" into the passage! This is not so! Messiah the Prince" means the same thing in both verses, Jesus the Messiah and Prince of peace! It was "the people of the prince who is to come shall destroy the city and the sanctuary". Jesus said that He, the King, would "send His armies, destroy those murderers, and burn their city" (Matthew 22:7)! The Roman armies were "His armies" carrying out His judgment. Remember that Nebuchadnezzar was referred to as "my servant" (Jeremiah 27:6), "Nebuchadnezzar the king of Babylon, my servant", not because he was a good guy, but because he was to be God's instrument in judgment, carrying about His purposes! The last verse in the passage is still referring to the messiah, when it says, "He shall confirm the covenant with MANY" (Daniel 9:27). Jesus referred to this in Matthew 28:20, when He said, "even as the Son of man came not to be ministered unto, but to minister, and to give his life a ransom for MANY."

We see this in Matthew 26:28 as well, "for this is my blood of the New Testament, which is shed for MANY for the remission of sins."

And Isaiah 53:11 tells of it.

"He shall see of the travail of his soul and shall be satisfied: by his knowledge shall my righteous servant justify MANY; for he shall bear their iniquities."

Hebrews 9:28 also affirms this,

"So Christ was once offered to bear the sins of MANY; and unto them that look for him shall he appear the second time without sin unto salvation."

This gospel went out and was confirmed to the many in those first years after the cross! It is very important to know that no teacher, prior to dispensationalism, and no commentator or scholar ever taught this passage to be in the future, but that it was clearly fulfilled in AD 70, when the Romans destroyed the city and the sanctuary (Daniel 9:26). It is only in this newly fabricated and discombobulated dispensational teaching, introduced primarily by Darby and Scofield, where Christians began to expect a worse and darker and darker future, which has become a self-fulfilling prophecy! This tribulation (Daniel 12:1, Matthew 24:21), occurred when Jesus said it would, in the first century, "This generation shall not pass, till all these things be fulfilled" (Matthew 24:34). PS, 21 comes before 34! Jesus brought us "everlasting righteousness" (Daniel 9:24) through His righteousness (2 Corinthians 5:21), in the "everlasting covenant" (Hebrews 13:20)! Again, the futurist understanding of Daniel's 70 weeks was never taught until the Premillennial Dispensational cult began propagating it as such in the last hundred plus years! The 70, 7-year periods of time, 490 years, began at the time of the command to rebuild the city of Jerusalem in Daniel 9:25, the Messiah being cut off and killed in 9:26, to confirming the new covenant to many, while bringing judgment upon the old covenant system as had been determined by Jesus in the Olivet Discourse.

Note that Jesus is connecting these numbers, 70 times 7, in relation to the complete forgiveness of God in Matthew 18:22.

The false concept of our day is that this final 7 years of Daniel's prophecy is found in a future "TRIBULATION PERIOD ". Let's examine this.

Dispensationalism teaches that there is either a future PRE-TRIBULATION, MID TRIBULATION, PRE-WRATH, or POST TRIBULATION rapture. None of the above is the correct answer. It is a PAST TRIBULATION, which occurred when Jesus said it would.

Jesus told his first century disciples, "And YOU shall be hated of all men for my name's sake: but he that endures to the end, the same shall be saved." (Matthew 10:22)

He then says the same thing to them, verbatim, in Matthew 24:9,13, "…and YOU shall be hated of all nations for my name's sake…But he that shall endure unto the end, the same shall be saved."

He then tells us when this tribulation would occur in verse 34 of the chapter, "This generation shall not pass, till ALL THESE THINGS be fulfilled" (Matthew 24:34).

Verse 21 is also describing the tribulation and is part of ALL THESE. "for then shall be GREAT TRIBULATION, such as was not since the beginning of the world to this time, no, nor ever shall be"

Matthew 24:21 is saying that this was the worst tribulation for the Old Covenant people in that land.

Is Jesus a false prophet, not the Messiah, nor God in the flesh, or did He prophesy accurately of the tribulation being in the lifetime of His disciples in the first century? This is because verse 21 comes before verse 34, "THIS GENERATION shall not pass, till all these things be fulfilled "(Mt.24:34)

You are given no other options!

John said that he was in the tribulation, "I John, your brother and fellow partaker IN THE TRIBULATION." (Revelation 1:9).

Note that the older manuscripts use the definite Greek article "ho" (the), The KJV manuscripts aren't as old and omit this word. Ironically, Darby includes it and says, "THE TRIBULATION".

Paul tells believers to not even get married at that time, because of "the present distress" (1 Corinthians 7:26), the tribulation.

So, the tribulation is past, and there is no RAPTURE disappearing act in our future! Jesus prayed that Christians would not be removed from the world, "I pray NOT that you take them out of the world…" (John 17:15). The four options we've been given are entirely man-made imaginations, not Holy Spirit inspired revelations!

A couple more passages that rapturists like to use is Revelation 4:1, where John and John alone is asked in the vision (Revelation 1:11) to "come up here" and see things from God's higher perspective. How this is forced to mean an airlift of millions from the planet is simply bizarre!

John 14:3 is another go to passage for the Bail worshippers, as in let's bail out of here.

John 14:3 "And if I go and prepare a place for you, I WILL COME (erchomai) again and receive you unto myself; that where I am, there ye may be also."

Let's consider the verse prior to gather the context of the entire chapter.

John 14:2 "In my Father's house are many MANSIONS (Mone) : if it were not so, I would have told you. I go to prepare a place for you."

The context of the chapter is really the dwelling place of the father. Even the famous verse, in John 14:6, is about this, "I am the way, the truth, and the life" is about coming TO THE FATHER."

"Mone" is the Greek work for mansions, which simply means, "a staying, abiding, dwelling, abode". It's really just a rich dwelling place. A wealthy Spanish dwelling is called "manor" in our day in relation to this word.

This rich dwelling place (mone) is in the Father's house (John 14:2).

We see this dwelling place revealed to us later in John 14.

John 14:23 "Jesus answered and said to him, "If anyone loves Me, he will follow My word; and My Father will love him, and WE WILL COME (erchomai) to him and make Our DWELLING (mone) with him."

The same two Greek words describing the same COMING (erchomai) and DWELLING PLACE (mone)as we see in John 14:2,3.

There are not two different comings and two different dwelling places in John 14:2,3 and John 14:23.

The same two Greek words are used at the beginning of the chapter, mone (John 14:2) and erchomai (John 14:3) and near the end of the chapter in John 14:23!

This does away with the sci-fi teleportation interpretation of the passage!

This rich "dwelling place" is revealed to us in

Ephesians 2:22 "in whom you also are being built together into a DWELLING OF GOD in the Spirit."

This place is in the Spirit, so there goes that Holy Spirit again, interpreting the Bible Spiritually, contrary to the natural mind of the Dispensational Pharisees of our day.

Here is that rich heavenly place as well.

Ephesians 2:6 "and raised us up with Him, and SEATED US WITH HIM IN THE HEAVENLY PLACES IN CHRIST JESUS".

This is secondary and not as prominent of a "place" as the natural mind's imagination gives us a physical teleportation to something greater in John 14:2,3.

The riches and wealth of God's dwelling place, "mone" in John 14:2,23 is not God's ultimate for the pharisaical mind, even though God reveals it multiple times.

Colossians 2:3 "that their hearts may be encouraged, having been knit together in love, and that they would attain to all the WEALTH (RICHES) that comes from the full assurance of understanding, resulting in a true knowledge of God's mystery, that is, Christ Himself, in whom are hidden all the TREASURES of wisdom and knowledge."

This wealth and these treasures are all chump change to the Pharisee, who assures us of a better kingdom that comes by observation (Luke 17:20,21).

Here is that same place, which the Pharisees say is temporal and lesser than their kingdom.

Colossians 3:3 "For you have died, and your life is HIDDEN WITH CHRIST IN GOD"

Again, this hiding place is a minor place "IN GOD", for the natural mind. There is to be a better dwelling place in Jesus someday, when John 14:2,3 happens in our future. The current Hiding Place isn't really all that for the futurist Pharisee!

Psalm 32:7 "YOU ARE MY HIDING PLACE; You keep me from trouble; You surround me with songs of deliverance. Selah"

A second class hiding place in futurism.

So, according to futurism, the "RICHES OF THE GLORY OF HIS INHERITANCE IN THE SAINTS" (Ephesians 1:18) and as you "LET THE WORD OF CHRIST RICHLY DWELL WITHIN YOU" (Colossians 3:16), is all of a much lesser value in "another gospel" (Galatians 1:6-9) offered to you in futurism's interpretation of John 14:2,3!

With the tribulation behind us, then all focus should be on the kingdom of God before us.

Dispensationalism teaches that we are presently living at the end of time, with the world about to end. It refers to this time as "THE CHURCH AGE". And within that age, we are in the final era of the church age, being the church in Laodicea. It was an unfaithful, weak, and lukewarm church, so let's all go fulfill our destiny in being such!

The youth, who are brought up in the church, are leaving after they come of age at the rate of nearly 80%! And the theology I'm presenting here is dangerous? The youth are offered a darker and darker forecast, a takeover by the devil, around which time they are to evacuate in a disappearing act, then everyone and everything gets nuked, now go take on the day! The youth long for a challenge and to see revolutionary change as a result. What better news for them to hear that the takeover of their family, community, country and world is in God's heart, mind, and plan? We've given them lies and an evil report through our erroneous false teaching! They've been given the gospel of death! Tell everybody they can do a Hale Bop (suicide cult) disappearing act, and that when you die you'll go to heaven.

The church is adhering to this evil report! The principal of taking the land, little by little (Exodus 23:30), the increase of His kingdom (Isaiah 9:7) goes out the door with a predetermined "prophecy", of a takeover by an antichrist! Therefore, long term goals are lost! The left operates in the principle of taking the land little by little through incrementalism. How many Law Schools do evangelical Christians have? Last I counted, it was about 2! The left has hundreds, because their worldview has much more truth in it considering the future, it exists, which allows for long term planning! There are dozens of Catholic Law schools because they don't have dispensational teaching and can set long term goals! This doctrine of demons will have Christians cheering on the evil to take over, so that they can fly out of here and let the place get nuked! I've heard this reasoning with my very ears! Contrary to this thinking, consider the preterist preacher John Locke (1632-1704). He only laid the foundations for the entire Western World in his philosophy concerning private landownership as the primary right to allow for free market capitalism!

What one believes about the future,

effects what one does and how one does it! It also affects whether one does it at all! Today the church has the goals of one on death row, i.e. short-term goals! To have a Great Tribulation hanging over your head, in the back of your mind gives you a world view that affects you subconsciously about what you do and how you do it!

Let's examine the Holy Spirit's revelation of "The Church Age". "to Him be the glory in THE CHURCH and in Christ Jesus to all generations, AGE (Aion) WITHOUT END, Amen."

(Ephesians 3:21). This verse contradicts everything Dispensationalists are saying about a so-called church age! It is an AGE WITHOUT END! Yet, their teaching entirely focuses on an end of such! This New Covenant Kingdom is prophesied in Isaiah by saying, "Of the increase of His government and peace, there shall be NO END" (Isaiah 9:7)! Yet, dispensational teaching continues to emphasize "End Time" matters, to which God Himself says NO END! What a contradiction of men opposing the Spirit of God through their multi-billion-dollar "Prophetic" (Pathetic)   Industrial Complex!

This evil report (Number 13) goes in direct opposition of Isaiah 9:7 in another way as well. The verse speaks of "THE INCREASE OF HIS GOVERNMENT" knowing no end. This contradicts modern futurism being taught in our day that the darkness will get darker and the church's light will get lighter. If light increases, then darkness is expelled and decreases! You can't have it both ways, unless you have a schizophrenic double minded doctrine, which is what you have with futurism! By the way, do examine first century Roman morality and you will see its darkness far exceeding that of our day.

One of the reasons allowing for the continuation of Dispensationalism amongst Christians is because leaders insulate themselves by being surrounded with Yes Men and Fanboys. Again, the authority of God comes through the truth of His word alone, not through the order of man and his illegitimate positions of power. It is the anointing and true revelation of His word that establishes the authority of God.

CHAPTER 6

MATTHEW 24 IS NOT KNOCKING AT THE DOOR.

"Before you attempt to understand John's letter to the seven churches, you should know what Jesus taught John on the mount of Olives about the end of the age"

"So, if Jesus is teaching that everything will be fulfilled in "this generation," (Matthew 24:34) would it not make sense that everything should take place within the lifetime of Jesus' first disciples? Is not this the most literal and straight forward reading of the text?"

-R.C. Sproul

"And when those that believed in Christ had come thither from Jerusalem, then, as if the royal city of the Jews and the whole land of Judea were entirely destitute of holy men, the judgment of God at length overtook those who had committed such outrages against Christ and his apostles and totally destroyed that generation of impious men." (Ecclesiastical History, Book III, Ch. 5)

"When, then, we see what was of old foretold for the nations fulfilled in our day, and when the lamentation and wailing that was predicted for the Jews, and the burning of the Temple and its utter desolation, can also be seen even now to have occurred according to the prediction, surely we must also agree that the King who was prophesied, the Christ of God, has come, since the signs of His coming have been shown in each instance I have treated to have been clearly fulfilled."

"All this (Matthew 24) occurred in this manner in the second year of the reign of Vespasian [A.D. 70], according to the predictions of our Lord and Savior Jesus Christ.

"Now, our Lord has identified his predictions (Matt. xxiv. and Luke xxi.) with these of Daniel. In the former (ver. 14.) He says: " then shall the END come. When ye therefore shall see the abomination… spoken of by Daniel the prophet" (ix. 27; xii. 11.)…" then shall be great tribulation" (ver. 21. comp. Dan. ix. 26; xii. 1.) ', ver. 34, "This generation shall not pass till all these things be," i. e. commenced (comp. ver. 8.). In the latter (Luke xxi. ver. 22.) " These be the days of vengeance, that ALL THINGS which are written MAY BE FULFILLED" (i. e. in them). That the terms, latter days, last days, end of the world, ends of the world, the fulness of time, refer to the times of the Apostles, and those immediately subsequent to these, the Concordance, with the parallels marked in our common Bibles, will be sufficient to shew."

-Eusebius Caesarea (AD 263-339)

This gospel of the kingdom will be preached throughout the whole world, as a testimony to all nations; and the end will come." The sign of this final end time will be the downfall of Jerusalem.

-John Chrysostom (AD 347-407)

"The Kingly Prophet foretold the time of the end: "Verily I say unto you, All these things shall come upon this generation." It was before that generation had passed away that Jerusalem was besieged and destroyed. There was a sufficient interval for the full proclamation of the gospel by the apostles and evangelists of the early Christian Church, and for the gathering out of those who recognized the crucified Christ as their true Messiah. Then came the awful end, which the Savior foresaw and foretold, and the prospect of which wrung from his lips and heart the sorrowful lament that followed his prophecy of the doom awaiting his guilty capital."

-Charles Spurgeon

"Verily I say unto you, This generation shall not pass, till all these things be fulfilled. This generation of men now living shall not pass till all these things be done - The expression implies that great part of that generation would be passed away, but not the whole. Just so it was. For the city and temple were destroyed thirty-nine or forty years after."

-John Wesley

"This prophecy does not relate to evils that are distant, and which posterity will see after the lapse of many centuries, but which are now hanging over you, and ready to fall in one mass, so that there is no part of it which the present generation will not experience…Christ informs them, that before a single generation shall have been completed, they will learn by experience the truth of what he has said. For within fifty years the city was destroyed and the temple was razed, the whole country was reduced to a hideous desert."

-John Calvin

"It is to me a wonder how any man can refer part of the foregoing discourse [Matt. 24] to the destruction of Jerusalem, and part to the end of the world, or any other distant event, when it is said so positively here in the conclusion, All these things shall be fulfilled in this generation".

-Thomas Newton

This chapter contains a prediction of the utter destruction of the city and temple of Jerusalem, and the subversion of the whole political constitution of the Jews; and is one of the most valuable portions of the new covenant Scriptures, with respect to the evidence which it furnishes of the truth of Christianity. Everything which our Lord foretold should come on the temple, city, and people of the Jews, has been fulfilled in the most correct and astonishing manner...."

—Adam Clarke

"The words relating to a personal return of Jesus are to be taken as pointing to the destruction of Jerusalem [in AD 70] (Matt. x. 23, xvi. 28)."

-Philip Schaff (1819 - 1893)

"The last days WERE the last days of the old covenant age" ("Dominion", chapter 3)

-C Peter Wagner

"The Olivet Discourse (Matthew 24, Mark 13, Luke 21).. is a prophecy of the destruction of Jerusalem in A.D. 70" (Paradise Restored, p. 224)

-David Chilton

"If Jesus and the early church used the relevant language in the same way as their contemporaries, it is highly unlikely that they would have been referring to the actual end of the world, and highly likely that they would have been referring to events within space–time history which they interpreted as the coming of the kingdom."

-NT Wright

"And Verily I say unto you; and urge you to observe it, as absolutely necessary in order to understand what I have been saying, That this generation of men now living shall not pass away until all these things be fulfilled, for what I have foretold concerning the destruction of the Jewish state is so near at hand, that some of you shall live to see it accomplished with a dreadful exactness."

-Phillip Doddridge

"But of wars in Jerusalem is He speaking; for it is not surely of those without, and everywhere in the world; for what did they care for these? And besides, He would thus say nothing new, if He were speaking of the calamities of the world at large, which are happening always. For before this, were wars, and tumults, and fightings; but He speaks of the Jewish wars coming upon them at no great distance, for henceforth the Roman arms were a matter of anxiety. Since then these things also were sufficient to confound them, He foretells them all.

Therefore, He saith, they shall come not by themselves or at once, but with signs. For that the Jews may not say, that they who then believed were the authors of these evils, therefore hath He told them also of the cause of their coming upon them. "For verily I say unto you," He said before, "all these things shall come upon this generation," having made mention of the stain of blood on them. "

-Chrysostom (AD 375)

"But our Master did not prophesy after this fashion; but, as I have already said, being a prophet by an inborn and every-flowing Spirit, and knowing all things at all times, He confidently set forth, plainly as I said before, sufferings, places, appointed times, manners, limits. Accordingly, therefore, prophesying concerning the temple, He said: "See ye these buildings? Verily I say to you, There shall not be left here one stone upon another which shall not be taken away [Matt. 24:3]; and this generation shall not pass until the destruction begin [Matt. 24:34]. . . ." And in like manner He spoke in plain words the things that were straightway to happen, which we can now see with our eyes, in order that the accomplishment might be among those to whom the word was spoken.63 (Clementine Homilia, 3:15. See Roberts and Donaldson, Ante-Nicene Fathers, 8:241.)

-Clement of Alexandria (A.D.150-215)

"Some evangelicals – being made unnecessarily uncomfortable by these statements and wishing to salvage their status as true predictions of the Second Coming – have interpreted the expression "this generation" in various ways. The phrase has been made out to mean " this race," or "the generation that sees the signs of the Second Coming," etc. – despite the fact that Jesus spoke of "this generation" in at least four other verses in Matthew in which no meaning can be ascribed to the expression but "those living at this time." In any case, the similar phrase, "there are some standing here who shall not taste death till…" is not so easy to reinterpet. Both passages seem to tell us that something called the coming of the Son of man was to occur within the generation of Jesus' followers." (Revelation, p.24)

-Steve Gregg

"Jesus made it clear what GENERATION would be charged with the Matthew 24 judgements...the generation that saw signs, wonders and miracles with their own eyes and still crucified Christ anyway. How long is a generation? Remember, all I have done here is point out the obvious that is often overlooked by the "prophecy teachers.

That generation did not pass away until everything in Matthew 24 was fulfilled."

-Kris Vallotton

The Church had these great pillars of the past to stand on their shoulders and build the kingdom. Instead leaders rejected them as they were seduced by C.I.Scofield and his reference bible. These pillars were the Reformers and their descendants. Scofield was a convicted conman, who left his wife and two daughters, and I believe ran off with his secretary, was a hard drinker, a lawyer and a corrupt politician. And , it appears that he had to have been payed and assisted writing the first bible of its type, with massive amounts of notes on each page telling you what the passage means. This assistance would be needed, because the project took only 2 years! He took John Nelson Darby's work and propagated it. Darby was highly educated, I believe he spoke five languages. Scofield's Bible was signed, sealed and ready to seduce in 1909!

Every teacher I've ever heard has said that Matthew 24, Mark 13, and Luke 21, The Olivet Discourse, is saying the same thing that the book of Revelation is saying. This discourse is much simpler to understand, as the book of Revelation is a vision, "what you SEE write in a book". (Revelation 1:11). The vision is highly symbolic! Matthew 24 is the same events as Revelation's 22 chapters. There is much less symbolism, though there is a bit of prophetic and apocalyptic language that must be interpreted in light of the Old Testament, which much of it is being quoted from. The primary rule in interpreting scripture, is to let scripture interpret scripture, to let the case of truth be built. And the more scripture to back up a point, the stronger the foundation is for that point.

It is Matthew 24 that was the entire contents for Hal Lindsay's, "The Late Great Planet Earth". This book's 30 million copies infiltrated the Jesus movement and neutered it! The gospel became a 2 for 1 special, one, receive Jesus, two, get raptured, and accept that the culture is presently to get darker and darker, and worse and worse! But wait, that's not all, Israel is a fulfillment of bible prophecy, which is much more exciting and something to be passionate about in our day than Jesus is! This isn't how it is said, but the passion and no compromise on the subject, the deal breaker, is truly greater in the hearts and minds of many believers!

As we've examined, the church age has "NO END" , according to Ephesians 3:21, and the New Covenant kingdom has "NO END", according to Isaiah 9:7, so what end is Jesus talking about in Matthew 24:3, "Tell us of the sign of your coming, and of THE END OF THE AGE"?

This "end" is in the context of the desolation of the Old Covenant temple, "Your HOUSE is left unto you desolate" (Matthew 23:38).

CHAPTER 7

MATTHEW 24:1-3, 34

THE TEMPLE OF DOOM

Matthew 24:1

"And Jesus went out and departed from the temple: and his disciples came to him for to shew him the buildings of THE TEMPLE."

Matthew 24:2

"And He said to them, "Do YOU not see all these things? Truly I say to YOU, not one stone here will be left upon another, which will not be torn down."

So, we have the end of the age in the next verse (3) in the context of the desolation of the temple. That is, the end of the Old Covenant age.

Let's continue to examine this, who is asking? It is "His disciples" (24:1), "tell US" (24:3). Jesus then answers THEM, (24:4) "And Jesus answered and said to them, "See to it that no one misleads YOU."

YOU, not "THEM" on the internet in 2000 years! Jesus says "THEM", when He is referring to others, not disciples, when He says, "Neither pray I for these alone, but for THEM also which shall believe on me through their word;" (John 17:20).

In this chapter, Matthew 24, Jesus assures His first century disciples whom He is warning concerning these things by saying "YOU" about 10 times, as we will see! The very next verse reveals this (24:4),

"And Jesus answered and said unto them, Take heed that no man deceive YOU."

The temple and its destruction is the context of the passage! After Jesus said, "Your HOUSE is left to you desolate" (23:38), this prompted His disciples to point out the magnitude and majesty of the temple that He just declared would become desolate. Matthew 24:1 "Jesus left the temple area and was going on His way when His disciples came up to POINT OUT the temple buildings to Him." Their response was almost saying, "are you sure about that happening to all of this?"

Answer, yes!

Matthew 24:2 "But He responded and said to them, "DO YOU NOT SEE all these things? Truly I say to you, not one stone here will be left upon another, which will not be torn down."

This is what sparks the disciples question concerning Jesus' COMING judgment upon it, and the end of the old covenant AGE in 24:3!

Eschatology is all about the temple, the dwelling place of God. The Old Covenant temple was coming down, and the New Covenant temple would take its place. Jesus was the last temple left standing.

Hebrews 9:8 "the Holy Spirit indicating this, that the way into the Holiest of All was not yet made manifest while the first tabernacle was still standing."

The WAY into the holiest of all is Jesus! It was not clear, "made manifest" what temple the people were to serve. It was to be the temple of Jesus Christ alone. After the first one went down, it became clear what temple was to be served. Christians weren't sure how much of the Old Covenant observances and sacrifices they were to adhere to. It became clear after AD 70. Jesus was the last temple standing!

Revelation 21:22 "I saw no temple in it, for the Lord God the Almighty and the Lamb are its temple."

For the natural minded ones talking about a physical city in the Middle East, cube shaped, hovering, etc, the Holy Spirit says that it's rather a Spiritual temple.

The Holy Spirit gets very spiritual concerning this temple.

Ephesians 2:21,22 "in whom the whole building, being fitted together, is GROWING INTO A HOLY TEMPLE IN THE LORD, in whom you also are being built together into a dwelling of God in the Spirit."

He says that the stones making up this temple are actually people.

1 Peter 2:5 "you also, as living stones, are being BUILT UP AS A SPIRITUAL HOUSE, a holy priesthood, to offer up spiritual sacrifices acceptable to God through Jesus Christ."

The Holy Spirit interpreting the Bible spiritually again!

Revelation 3:12 "He who overcomes, I WILL MAKE HIM A PILLAR IN THE TEMPLE OF MY GOD, and he shall go out no more. I will write on him the name of My God and the name of the city of My God, the New Jerusalem, which comes down out of heaven from My God. And I will write on him My new name." Saying that the temple of Jesus Himself is secondary to your carnal cubed shaped imaginary one in the Middle East boarders on blasphemy!

A person is made into a pillar in this temple! How many temples does God have?

Matthew 24:3 "And as he sat upon the mount of Olives, the disciples came unto him privately, saying, Tell US when shall these things be? and what shall be the sign of thy COMING (Parousia), and of the end of the age (Aion)?"Note the Greek word for "coming" is Parousia, which means; "Coming presence". It is NOT defined as coming bodily, physically, and visibly! And "Aion" means; "Age", not "world" as the King James gets this wrong here.

Mark reveals that this is not three separate issues that Jesus is being asked, "Tell US, when shall these things be? and what shall be the sign when ALL THESE THINGS SHALL BE FULFILLED?" (Mark 13:4). The synoptic gospels all follow this question immediately with the same response, "Take heed that no man deceives you" (Matthew 24:4, Mark 13:5, Luke 21:8).

They are all asking Jesus the same question, as the answer is exactly the same in all three accounts! Remember to interpret scripture with scripture.

Let's back-in to the entire chapter now with going ahead to verse 34, before we continue going verse by verse with verse 4.

We just read in verse 3 about Jesus' coming, when THESE THINGS would be FULFILLED.

Matthew 24:34 says, "Verily I say unto YOU, THIS GENERATION shall not pass, till ALL THESE THINGS be fulfilled." Therefore, the happenings of verses 4-33 take place when verse 34 says they do, within "THIS GENERATION"! Modern day futurism contorts this verse like there's no tomorrow, pun intended. No amount of exegesis (extracting from the text) is expended in futurism, you will only see great efforts of eisegesis reading into the text). They will often change the wording of a verse to force it to mean what their futurist system of interpretation wants it to mean. They will say, "THE (changing "this") generation that sees these things (4 added words) will not pass, till all these things be fulfilled". "This" is a very important word here. It is a "near demonstrative". If I say, "This computer" that I'm using, which is nearest to me", as opposed to "that computer", not nearest to me and further away, the understanding is clear. Such is the simple understanding of a near demonstrative, "This generation", which is nearest to me, as opposed to one that is further away. Another variation used is "That (changing "this") generation, which sees these things (4 added words), will not pass, till all these things be fulfilled". Again, this computer nearest me, as opposed to that computer, which is not nearest to me, but further away.

A few verses before Matthew 24, remember that there are no inspired chapter breaks, Jesus says to the pharisees, after calling them murderers and snakes, "that upon you may come all the righteous blood shed upon the earth, from the blood of Zacharias son of Barachias, whom ye slew between the temple and the altar. Verily I say unto you, All these things shall come upon THIS GENERATION" (Matthew 23:35,36). No one questions what generation Jesus is referring to here, as blood was to be "required of THIS GENERATION" (Luke 11:51). Blood would "come upon THIS GENERATION" (Matthew 23:36)! Therefore, "THIS GENERATION" can't mean something different here in Matthew 23:36 than what it means in the next chapter, Matthew 24:34, "THIS GENERATION shall not pass, till all these things be fulfilled"! Another attempt is made when futurists change "This generation" to "This Race", which no translations do because the Greek word for generation is "Genea", and it is "Genos" that can mean race. Of the nearly 40 times that Genea is used in the New Testament, futurist teachers will say that the word always means a generation of people living together at the same time, but the 3 times its used in the Olivet Discourse (Mt.24, Mk.13, Lk.21) it means "race".

Let's examine the New Testament usage of "Generation" and how "THIS GENERATION" is used over a dozen times in the New Testament.

Matthew 3:7 "…O GENERATION of vipers, who hath warned you to flee from the wrath to come?

Matthew 11:16 "But whereunto shall I liken THIS GENERATION?

Matthew 12:41 "The men of Nineveh shall rise in judgment with THIS GENERATION…"

Matthew 12:42 "The queen of the south shall rise in judgment with THIS GENERATION…"

Matthew 12:45 "Even so shall it be also unto "THIS WICKED GENERATION."

Matthew 16:4 "A WICKED AND ADULTEROUS GENERATION seeketh after a sign…"

Matthew 23:33 "Ye serpents, ye GENERATION OF VIPERS,"

Matthew 23:36 "All these things shall come upon THIS GENERATION."

Matthew 24:34 "THIS GENERATION shall not pass, till all these things be fulfilled."

Mark 8:12 "There shall no sign be given unto THIS GENERATION…"

Mark 8:38 "…ashamed of me and of my words in THIS ADULTEROUS, AND SINFUL GENERATION…"

Mark 9:19 "He answered him, and saith, O FAITHLESS GENERATION…"

Luke 7:31 "Whereunto then shall I liken the men of THIS GENERATION?"

Luke 9:41 "…O FAITHLESS AND PERVERSE GENERATION."

Luke 11:30 "…as Jonas was a sign unto the Ninevites, so shall also the Son of man be to THIS GENERATION."

Luke 11:31 "The queen of the south shall rise up in judgment with the men of THIS GENERATION."

Luke 11:32 "The men of Nineve shall rise up in the judgment with the men of THIS GENERATION."

This is communicated by Jesus concerning Jonah and His own resurrection, a first century event!

Matthew 12:39-41"But he answered and said unto them, An evil and adulterous generation seeketh after a sign; and there shall no sign be given to it, but the sign of the prophet Jonas: for as Jonas was three days and three nights in the whale's belly; so shall the Son of man be three days and three nights in the heart of the earth. The men of Nineveh shall rise in judgment with this generation and shall condemn it: because they repented at the preaching of Jonas; and, behold, a greater than Jonas is here."

Luke 11:50 "That the blood of all the prophets, which was shed from the foundation of the world, may be required of THIS GENERATION."

Luke 11:51 "…the blood…It shall be required of THIS GENERATION."

Luke 17:25 "But first must he suffer many things and be rejected of THIS GENERATION."

Acts 2:40 "…Save yourselves from THIS PERVERSE GENERATION."

Hebrews 3:9,10 "…forty years. Wherefore, I was grieved with THAT GENERATION." God clarifies here that He is NOT speaking about "THIS" PRESENT GENERATION, by using "THAT" GENERATION within the context of "your fathers.".

P.S. Does "THIS GENERATION" mean something different in Matthew 23:36, where Jesus pronounces judgment upon the murderous snake's ruling Israel in the first century, than it does in the very next chapter, which begins four verses later where that chapter's judgments are given the same timeline in Matthew 24:34?

"THIS GENERATION shall NOT pass, till all these things be fulfilled" (Matthew 24:34)!

If this simple truth were believed, that the last days WERE the last days of the Old Covenant age, Latter Day Saints (Mormonism), Jehovahs Witnesses, and much of Islam would be no more!

Timing is everything and we must connect the timing of the Olivet Discourse, Matthew 24, Mark 13, Luke 21, with that of the book of Revelation. "This generation" is the same time indicator as are "soon/shortly" (Gk.Tachos) in Revelation 1:1, and it is "at hand/near" (Engys) in Revelation 1:3, 22:10.

There is no way to stretch the definition and New Testament usages of these words to mean thousands of years later!

Revelation 1:1 "The Revelation of Jesus Christ, which God gave Him to show to His bond-servants, the things which must SOON take place; and He sent and communicated it by His angel to His bond-servant John,"

SOON/SHORTLY, Tachos, takh'-os; from the same as G5036; a brief space (of time), i.e. (with G1722 prefixed) in haste: quickly, shortly, speedily.

Acts 25:4 "But Festus answered that Paul should be kept at Caesarea, and that he himself was going there SHORTLY (Tachos)."

Is there any way to make Festus' trip out to mean something that would take place thousands of years later?

How is it that futurists are staunch literalists, but are not literal on this plane and simple definition of "soon/shortly" (Tachos)?

NEAR/AT HAND, Engys, eng-goos'; from a primary verb ἄγχω áncho (to squeeze or throttle; akin to the base of G43); near (literally or figuratively, of place or time):—from , at hand, near, nigh (at hand, unto), ready.

Hebrews 8:13 "In that He says, "A new covenant," He has made the first obsolete. Now what is becoming obsolete and growing old is READY TO VANISH AWAY (Engys)."

This is the exact timing, in both passages, of the passing away of the Old Covenant temple, city, and nation in AD 70.

Revelation 1:1 "things which must SOON (Tachos) take place"

Hebrews 8:13 "In that He says, "A new covenant," He has made the first obsolete. Now what is becoming obsolete and growing old is READY TO VANISH AWAY (Engys)."

The Old Covenant system was still going here in Hebrews 8, but not for long as AD 70 was approaching.

Really think this one through! God is very logical, as He is the "Logos", where we get the word logic from.

John 2:13 "The Passover of the Jews was NEAR (Engys), and Jesus went up to Jerusalem."

Is there any way to stretch the timing of this Passover out to our day?

What did the words "near" and "soon" mean to the original audience, those to whom the book of Revelation was written to?

Revelation 1:4 "John, TO the seven churches which are in Asia…"

Consider God's prophetic words used to give a specific timeline in Ezekiel 12.

The people are falsely believing that the timing of the prophecy with the attitude that "The days are prolonged" (Ezekiel 12:22), "The vision that he sees is for many days to come, and he prophesies of the times that are far off" (Ezekiel 12:27). God corrects the timing misunderstanding by saying, "The days are at hand/near" (Ezekiel 12:23), "it shall no more be prolonged/delayed, for in your days, O rebellious house, will I say the word, and will perform it…" (Ezekiel 12:25), "none of my words will be prolonged any more, but the word I have spoken shall be done, says The Lord" (Ezekiel 12:28). So "at hand/near" and "no more prolonged" can't mean thousands of years off, any more than, "far off, prolonged/delayed" can mean tomorrow! Words have to mean something!

When God says, "WITH THE LORD a day is as a thousand years, and a thousand years is as one day" (2 Peter 3:8), this is the perspective of God, who is outside of time! This is not talking about man's perspective of time! Why would God then communicate to man and say, "THE CAPTIVITY (70 years) IS LONG" (Jeremiah 29:28)? Is it long for God, or for man who is in time? Also note, in 2 Peter 3 here, that the "last days (of the old covenant age) mockers", where Old Testament Jews, believing their system would continue, "for ever since the fathers (Jewish fathers) fell asleep, all things continue as they were…" (2 Peter 3:3,4).

Timing is everything, and the book of Revelation has the prophetic time indicators of "soon", and "at hand/near" (1:1,3,22:10). Note that Revelation in 22:10, John is instructed to "SEAL NOT the sayings of the prophecy of this book, for the time is "AT HAND". Daniel is told to do the exact opposite in his book, which prophecies are talking about the same things, yet they're nearly 600 years into Daniel's future, "SEAL THE BOOK, even to the time of the end" (Daniel 12:4)! "Go

49

your way. Daniel; for the words are SEALED UP until the time of the end" (not "end of time", but time of the end of the Old Covenant age). -Daniel 12:9

The prophecy/book was not for Daniel's day, "SEAL UP THE VISION, for it refers to many days in the future" (Daniel 8:26). Again, the timing words in these two prophetic books are exactly the opposite! "SEAL UP" and "SEAL NOT" (Daniel 12:4/Revelation 22:10) are prophetic time indicating words that have to mean something!

So, God knows how to tell time! Thanks, Don Preston for writing, "Can God tell time?"

Hebrews 10:37 "For yet a very little while he that comes WILL COME and WILL NOT DELAY."

Same COMING with the same timing as Matthew 10:23,16:28, 24:3,30,34).

Matthew 24:48 "But and if that evil servant shall say in his heart, My Lord DELAYS His COMING".

It is the futurist that delays Jesus' coming by 2K years!

For more timing words, do a study on the New Testament Greek word, "Mello", which means "about to".

2 Timothy 4.1 "I charge you therefore before God and the Lord Jesus Christ, who *will* ("Mello", is about to) judge the living and the dead at His appearing and His kingdom:"

We see the time frame given to us unequivocally clear in Luke 21:8 and 1 Peter 4:7.

Luke 21:8 "And He said: "Take heed that you not be deceived. For many will come in My name, saying, 'I am He,' and, 'The time has drawn NEAR.' Therefore do not go after them."

Here, we see that "NEAR" could be preached to mislead someone prematurely.

And the next verse eradicates futurism from existence!

Peter is writing nearly 40 years later and says that now things are near!

1 Peter 4:7 "The end of all things is NEAR…"

Their entire world, their nation, capital city, and temple were all bout to be destroyed, as God was "about to (Mello) judge the living and the dead" , which is 2 verses prior in 1 Peter 4:5. Consider Daniel 12:1-4 here. This is explained thoroughly later in this book in chapter 25.

This timeline given to us in Luke 21:8 and 1 Peter 4:7 is also seen in the countdown of the last days.

Acts 2:17, 1 Timothy 4:1, and Hebrews 1:2, all speak of,

"THE LAST DAYS".

John 6:40 refers to,

"THE LAST DAY" (NOT 24 hours)!

1 John 2:18 says that it is now,

"THE LAST HOUR" (NOT 60 minutes)!

Similarly, Matthew 24:3 speaks of the future, "THEN, at the end of the age", if you will.

"END OF THE AGE"

Where 30 something years later, Hebrews 9:26 says,

"But NOW, ONCE AT THE END OF THE AGE".

We see this also in,

1 Corinthians 10:11 "Now all these things happened unto them for ensamples: and they are written for our admonition, UPON WHOM THE ENDS OF THE AGE ARE COME".

When it's understood that these prophecies were unquestionably fulfilled in our past, one avenue that is sometimes taken then is, "Double Fulfillment ".

Are we to look to Bethlehem in our day to see Micah 5:2 fulfilled again? Yet, the application of Christ being formed in us is endless (Galatians 4:19).

Are we to looking to Calvary for the Psalm 22 and Isaiah 53 prophecies to be fulfilled again? No, but the application of the cross in our lives is endless.

Neither are we to see Jesus words to mean, "This generation shall not pass, till all these things be fulfilled, and then fulfilled again in 2K years in another generation" (NOT Matthew 23:34).

There is no need for Double Minded fulfillment! It is finished!

CHAPTER 8

MATTHEW 24:4,5

MISLEADERS AND DECEPTION

Matthew 24:4

"And Jesus answered and said to them, "See to it that no one MISLEADS YOU."

Matthew 24:5

"For many shall come in my name, saying, I am Christ; and shall deceive many."

This deception is revealed in Acts 5:36,37 "For before these days rose up Theudas, boasting himself to be somebody; to whom a number of men, about four hundred, joined themselves: who was slain; and all, as many as obeyed him, were scattered, and brought to nought. After this man rose up Judas of Galilee in the days of the taxing, and drew away much people after him: he also perished; and all, even as many as obeyed him, were dispersed."

Jerome, Iranaeus, Eusebius, and Josephus go into detail of such false messiahs in this passage as well as what we read in Acts 8:9-11, "But there was a certain man, called Simon, which before time in the same city used sorcery, and bewitched the people of Samaria, giving out that himself was some great one: to whom they all gave heed, from the least to the greatest, saying, This man is the great power of God. And to him they had regard, because that of long time he had bewitched them with sorceries."

CHAPTER 9

MATTHEW 24:6

WARS

Matthew 24:6

"And ye shall hear of WARS AND RUMORS OF WARS: see that ye be not troubled: for all these things must come to pass, but the end is not yet."

Let's pause for just a second and remember who Jesus is talking to, face to face? He is talking to "YOU," first century disciples! They were experiencing what historians referred to as "Pax Romana", meaning, Roman Peace", it was "The Age of Peace". Rome was a world-governing empire that seemed unshakable as it quickly put every threat under its feet. But Jewish uprisings began to occur often, being put down with staggering losses culminating with the Jewish war in AD 70 when the nation was leveled and burned to the ground with over 1.2 million Jews killed. Josephus records that instability in the empire broke out as there were civil wars resulting from 4 emperors in the space of 2 years, Nero, Galba, Otho, and Vitellius. Tacitus speaks of "The War in Britain", "The War in Armenia", "Disturbances in Germany", "intrigues among the Parthians", "Insurrections in Gaul", and "commotions in Africa and in Thrace".

200 MILLION MAN ARMY?

Note that the red horse in Revelation 6:4 symbolizes war and bloodshed. And the verse we're expanding on here in Matthew 24:6 does not say that the wars will be the most massive in history, but simply that there will be wars period.

The "200-million-man army in Revelation 9:16 uses the Greek words "Dyo Myrias Murias". Old Strong's concordances don't even have the words for the number here, and a Greek Interlinear is needed. "Dyo", means two, and Myrais, Myrais, the same word used twice, is defined as "a myriad, an indefinite number, an innumerable amount". The word simply means a lot, doubled. 200 million is cancelled out mathematically in this definition. I was taught that 200 million proved the futurist view, because the entire earth's population was only 200 million in the first century, meaning that an army this size was not possible then. Just another miscalculation of futurism. Revelation has an army, "the number of whom is as the sand of the sea" (Revelation 20:8)! Futurists don't try to count such, because it doesn't fit their fable. This is what imagination, not revelation does. It throws paint at the canvas and then an "enlightened" artist interprets it to mean what he wants it to mean!

This same number, which is wrongfully put at 200 million, fails as this army is on horseback in Revelation 9:16. There are only 60 million horses on the planet today. Is this army riding 3 or 4 soldiers on each horse, with 100 percent of the globe's horses gathered in one place? Do we fight battles on Horses today? And these "200 million" (Not) soldiers on horseback are coming from China, according to futurist prophecy experts. So, they choose to put four on a horse, travel over the highest mountain range in the world, the Himalayas, and then all the way to the Middle East, in an era of massive military cargo planes, please!

While we're looking at false numbers in Revelation 9, let's examine a couple more verses that sensationalists use to propagate their "gospel" of doom

Revelation 9:15 "And the four angels were loosed, which were prepared for an hour, and a day, and a month, and a year, for TO SLAY THE THIRD PART OF MEN.

Revelation 9:18 *"By these three was THE THIRD PART OF MEN killed, by the fire, and by the smoke, and by the brimstone, which issued out of their mouths."*

This is not referring to 1/3 part of "mankind" on the planet, any more than Acts 2:17 is.

"And it shall be in the last days, 'God says, 'That I will pour out My Spirit ON ALL MANKIND; And your sons and your daughters will prophesy, And your young men will see visions, And your old men will have dreams;"

Let's ask when, where, and who are the players?

WHEN? The book of Revelation's prophecy was to occur "shortly" (Tachos) and the time was "at hand/near (Engys) -Revelation 1:1,3,22:10). The same prophecy as the Olivet discourse in Matthew 24 with the same timeline, "This generation shall not pass, till all these things be fulfilled" (Matthew 24:34).

WHERE? The Olivet discourse tells us that the judgment is upon Jerusalem, and that Christians are given instructions on what to do when it was occurring.

Luke 21:20,21, Mt.24:15,16) "But when you see JERUSALEM SURROUNDED by armies, then know that its desolation is near. Then let those who are in Judea FLEE to the mountains, let those who are in the midst of her depart, and let not those who are in the country enter her."

The book of Revelation identifies "THE GREAT CITY, BABYLON as "THE CITY WHERE OUR LORD WAS CRUCIFIED" (Revelation 11:8), which Luke tells us is Jerusalem (Luke 13:33).

The Great City, Babylon is mentioned nearly a dozen times in Revelation. I cite them all in this book in chapter 17.

WHO? The men, or mankind if you'd like, IN THE CITY! Location, location, location!

Revelation 11:13 "In the same hour there was a great earthquake, and A TENTH OF THE CITY FELL. In the earthquake seven thousand people were killed, and the rest were afraid and gave glory to the God of heaven."

Clearly stating that the prophecy concerns A CITY here! This is the case, regardless of what your doom and gloom pastors of disasters might say! Revelation is a judgment upon "THE GREAT CITY/BABYLON", "THE CITY WHERE OUR LORD WAS CRUCIFIED" (Revelation 11:8), which is Jerusalem (Luke 13:33). Much more on this in chapter 17.

Remember that the book of Revelation speaks of events occurring upon the LAND as Young's Translation accurately translates the word "Ge" as the land, not the globe!

CHAPTER 10

MATTHEW 24:7

WARS AND RUMORS OF WARS.

EZEKIEL 38 AND 39

The Gog and Magog war. A horse of course. The Mr. Ed led battle!

I will never forget a famous Calvary Chapel radio pastor, also a foreign policy expert, saying how that Russia was going to attack the modern nation of Israel for the purpose of taking the spoils of war, which includes "cattle" (Ezekiel 38:13). "All right, the cows, where are they, hand them over"! This message had the true Monty Python anointing on it!

This ancient battle was fought on horseback in Ezekiel 38 and 39. The book of Revelation alludes to Old Testament battles such as this one with Gog and Magog in Revelation 20:8. Again many Old Testament judgements are in the book, such as Egypt, Babylon, Sodom, Jezebel, Balaam, etc.

As for the Old Testament battle of Gog and Magog, Gary DeMar has a great book on this, "WHY THE END OF THE WORLD IS NOT IN YOUR FUTURE", which I believe has an updated title,"

THE GOG AND MAGOG END-TIME ALLIANCE ISRAEL, RUSSIA, AND SYRIA IN BIBLE PROPHECY".

Ezekiel 38:2 ""Son of man, set your face against Gog, of the land of Magog, the prince of ROSH, Meshech, and Tubal, and prophesy against him,"

Prophecy writers, often using good ghost writers, such as Hal Lindsey, have told us that ROSH here is referring to modern day Russia. This is because, the Hebrew word Rosh sounds like the English word Russia. The word actually means a position, such as head or captain. But close enough. One prophecy teacher, Doug Clark (TBN) would go on and on about how Tubal is modern day Turkey, Meshech is Moscow, and Gomer in verse 6 is Germany, with the mighty threat of Ethiopia's aggressive military in verse 5, wow! The guy was well spoken, and talked fast, so as an 18-year-old, I took him at his word.

In reality, all of these nations are within Esther 1:1.

Ezekiel 38:2,3 ""Son of man, set your face toward Gog of the land of Magog, the prince of ROSH, Meshech and Tubal, and prophesy against him and say, 'Thus says the Lord God, "Behold, I am against you, O Gog, prince of ROSH, Meshech and Tubal."

Again, the Hebrew word ROSH, means head, or chief, and has no connection with the English word Russia!

Ezekiel 38:4 "I will turn you around, put hooks into your jaws, and lead you out, with ALL YOUR ARMY, HORSES, AND HORSEMEN, all SPLENDIDLY CLOTHED, a great company with bucklers and shields, all of them handling swords."

Does this describe modern day warfare and weaponry? THEY ARE ON HORSEBACK, MAN!

I will make a side note here of the persecutors being SPLENDIDLY CLOTHED. Here is the definition of the name **Haman,** *Meaning*

Unique, MAGNIFICENT, ILLUSTRIOUS, Certainty, Trustworthy

Noisy Bunch *Etymology*

From Persian words meaning solitary, magnificent or illustrious.

From the verb אמן (*'aman***), to affirm or support.**

From the verb המה (*hama***), to be noisy.**

Ezekiel 38:8 "After many days thou shalt be visited: IN THE LATTER YEARS thou shalt come into THE LAND THAT IS BROUGHT BACK FROM THE SWORD, and is gathered out of many people, against the mountains of Israel, which have been always waste: but it is brought forth out of the nations, AND THEY SHALL DWELL SAFELY ALL OF THEM".

This battle takes place in later days, future days (**'achărîyth, future posterity),** not in Ezekiel's day. The type that it was, finds ultimate fulfillment in the New Covenant prophecy in Revelation 20:8, which was to be fulfilled "shortly", as the time was "at hand/near" (Revelation 1:1,3,22:10). Again, many Old Testament judgements are referenced in Revelation, Balaam, Jezebel, Egypt, Babylon, Sodom, and Armageddon, where just the mention of the valley of Megiddo struck images of the many, approximately 30, Old Testament battles that were fought there, where God's judgment was executed.

The scope of the latter years could technically be referring to the last days of the Old Covenant age, as this prophecy would occur in the latter half, I believe, maybe the latter third of that Old Covenant age.

The timing of Ezekiel's prophecy is that it was a word given at the time of the Babylonian captivity. They would be brought back to the land by the sword (Nehemiah 4:17), "THE LAND THAT IS BROUGHT BACK FROM THE SWORD" (Ezekiel 38:8). They would come back into the land at the time of the Medo-Persian empire. And modern day "prophecy" writers throw this prophecy, with such specifics, thousands of years into the future. And rest assured, in another thousand years the same natural man will continue to sensationalize such prophecies and say that they are happening "right before your eyes "!

At the time of this battle, Israel is DWELLING SAFELY, ALL OF THEM! Can you say, ANACHRONISM! Modern Israel is 180 degrees opposite of DWELLING SAFELY TODAY!

Only by being a satellite state, under a world governing empire (Medo-Persia) could Israel DWELL SAFELY.

Ezekiel 38:9 "Thou shalt ascend and COME like a storm, thou shalt be like a CLOUD to cover the land…"

Note that the words "COME" and "CLOUDS" prophetically denote an invading army, nothing to do with the natural elements.

Ezekiel 38:11 "You will say, 'I will go up against a land of UNWALLED VILLAGES; I will go to a peaceful people, who DWELL SAFELY, all of them DWELLING WITHOUT WALLS, and having neither bars nor gates'—"

Modern Israel has just completed one of the biggest and most expensive walls ever built! The West Bank Wall obliterates the forced futurist interpretation of the Ezekiel 38 and 39 battle! In modern Israel, the people do NOT DWELL SAFELY!

Esther reveals the battle where the people do live in UNWALLED VILLAGES.

Esther 9:19 "Therefore the Jews of the VILLAGES WHO DWELT IN THE UNWALLED TOWNS…"

Ezekiel 38:13 "…Art thou come TO TAKE A SPOIL? hast thou gathered thy company to take a prey? to carry away silver and gold, to take away cattle and goods, to take a great spoil?"

The motives of this invading army were "TO TAKE A SPOIL"! A primary spoil was to obtain Israel's "CATTLE"! Does any nation in our day invade another for the sake of taking their cattle? What an embarrassment "prophecy writers" have brought upon the Christian church!

Again, this is Monte Python stuff! "All right, hand em over, your cows and your strawberries, now!"

Ezekiel 38:16 "and thou shalt COME up against my people of Israel, as a CLOUD to cover the land; it shall be in the latter days, and I will bring thee against my land, THAT THE NATIONS MAY KNOW ME, when I shall be sanctified in thee, O Gog, before their eyes."

Let's begin to connect the dots with the book of Esther.

Esther 8:17 "And in every province, and in every city, whithersoever the king's commandment and his decree came, the Jews had joy and gladness, a feast and a good day. And MANY OF THE PEOPLE OF THE LAND BECAME JEWS; for the fear of the Jews fell upon them."

They came to KNOW God.

This verse also reveals that being a Jew, was always a faith matter, not a biological one! Persians became Jews that day!

Ezekiel 38:17 "Thus says the Lord God: "Are you he of whom I have spoken in former days by My servants the prophets of Israel, WHO PROPHESIED FOR YEARS IN THOSE DAYS THAT I WOULD BRING YOU AGAINST THEM?"

This was an existing nation, not one that wasn't formed yet! This rules out the modern nation of Russia! They had been prophesied about prior to this time. The modern Nation of Russia did not exist at this time.

Ezekiel 38:19,20 "…Surely in that day there shall be a GREAT SHAKING in the land of Israel; so that the FISH of the sea, and the BIRDS of the heaven, and the BEASTS of the field, and all CREEPING THINGS that creep upon the earth, and all the men that are upon the face of the earth, shall shake at MY PRESENCE, and the MOUNTAINS shall be thrown down, and the STEEP PLACES SHALL FALL , and every wall shall fall to the ground."

We can see the Dominion mandate, FISH, BIRDS and CREEPING THINGS (Genesis 1:26), and God's PRESENCE, as we remember the word "COMING" to mean COMING PRESENCE.

Also, this is not talking about the physical landscape when it talks about the MOUNTAINS, and the STEEP PLACES FALLING. We see the same prophetic language with John the Baptist.

Luke 3:5 "Every valley shall be filled And every MOUNTAIN and HILL BROUGHT LOW; The crooked places shall be made straight and the rough ways smooth;"

These prophecies are not talking about natural excavation, but spiritual transformation!

Earthquakes, though first the natural then the spiritual, speak of shaking things up in matters of authority and rule.

Hebrews 12:26-28 "whose voice then SHOOK the earth: but now he hath promised, saying, Yet once more I SHAKE not the earth only, but also heaven. And this word, yet once more, signified the removing of those THINGS that are SHAKEN, as of things that are made, that those things which CANNOT BE SHAKEN may remain. Wherefore we receiving A KINGDOM WHICH CANNOT BE MOVED, let us have grace, whereby we may serve God acceptably with reverence and godly fear:"

Luke 21:26 "men's hearts failing them for fear, and for looking after those things which are coming on the Roman World (Oikoumene): for THE POWERS OF HEAVEN SHALL BE SHAKEN."

Matthew 24:7 Earthquakes are the natural taking place first, then the spiritual (1 Cor.15:46) rule and authority is being shaken.

Ezekiel 38:21 Describes this battle as involving a "sword", not weapons of this or that type, but a SWORD! Not a battle in our day.

Ezekiel 38:22 Describes the battle as involving "HAILSTONES". We also see this in Revelation 16:21.

Ezekiel 39:2 (YLT) "" And have turned thee back, and enticed thee, And caused thee to come up FROM the sides of THE NORTH, And brought thee in against the mountains of Israel,"

Most every invasion into Israel has occurred FROM THE NORTH, as it is mountainous and allows for a downhill battle.

P.S. This verse is NOT saying that the invaders are from the north, but that the invasion comes from the north of the nation of Israel.

Consider this exact description in the following verses that describe an invasion FROM THE NORTH (Isaiah 41:25, Jeremiah 1:13-15, 4:6, 10:22,50:3, Ezekiel 26:7, Zachariah 2:6,7, Zephaniah 2:13). Ancient Israel new what this meant to the nation from its history. It meant THE DIRECTION from which the planned attack was to come from. Nothing to do with the location whereby the invading nation dwelt!

Ezekiel 39:9,10

"And they that dwell in the cities of Israel shall go forth, and shall set on fire and BURN THE WEAPONS, both the shields and the bucklers, the bows and the arrows, and the hand staves, and the spears, and they shall BURN THEM WITH FIRE SEVEN YEARS: SO THAT THEY SHALL TAKE NO WOOD OUT OF THE FIELD, NEITHER CUT DOWN ANY OUT OF THE FOREST; for they shall burn the weapons with fire: and they shall spoil those that spoiled them, and rob those that robbed them, saith the Lord GOD."

THE WEAPONS ARE MADE OF WOOD! Wooden weapons are ancient weapons! This is not describing modern weaponry! This is an ancient battle, as there are shields, spears, bows and arrows!

Ezekiel 38:11 "And it shall come to pass in that day, that I will give unto Gog a place there of graves in Israel, the valley of the passengers on the east of the sea: and it shall stop the noses of the passengers: and there shall they bury Gog and all his multitude: and they shall call it The valley of HAMON-GOG."

Here is the clear Esther connection. James B Jordan and Dr Phillip Kayser, Warren Nazaki, Michael Griego, and many others do some great work on this connection, as do many Jewish Scholars.

Haman was a descendant of the Amalekites/Agagites), an enemy of Israel. Agag, the original king of the Amalekites, is translated "Gog" in the Septuagint

(Numbers 24:7). Ham-an was promoted to the head, chief position in the Persian Empire in the early part of the 6th century BC.

Esther 3:10 "Then the king took his signet ring from his hand and gave it to Haman, the son of Hammedatha the Agagite, the enemy of the Jews."

One scholar puts it this way, "Ezekiel describes events from God's-eye-view, while Esther explains things from man's-eye-view."

Another implosion occurs for "prophecy experts" in our day saying that this future battle occurs BEFORE a rapture and the thousand-year reign. Revelation 20:8 reveals that its ultimate fulfillment occurs AFTER the thousand-year reign! Just a free wrench offered here to put in the fiction works of "Bible Prophecy writers.

Israel was under the rule of the Persian Empire, so there was no threat from foreign enemies. At this time Israel was DWELLING SAFELY and could live in UNWALLED VILLAGES (38:8,11). The circumstances don't fit concerning any other time frame. Trying to force this battle into the modern day is like attempting to put a square peg into a round hole!

Again, UNWALLED VILLAGES is specifically mentioned in Esther.

Esther 9:19 "Therefore the Jews of the villages who DWELT IN THE UNWALLED TOWNS..."

HAMON-GOG is mentioned twice, in Ezekiel 39:11,15.

HAMONAH is mentioned in Ezekiel 39:16.

Phillip Kayser says the following concerning the words Haman and Hamon spelling difference in his Esther series Sermon, "Haman's name appears in Ezekiel's prophecy as Hamon (39:11,15,16). Again, this slight change in pronunciation (which is common with other names) can be explained by the language differences. The phrase, "the valley of Hamon of Gog" would then be equivalent to Haman of Agag (or "Haman the Agagite")."

Ezekiel 39:12 "For seven months the house of Israel will be burying them, in order to cleanse the land."

This fits well with Esther mentioning of 75,000 of Israel's enemies being killed.

Esther 9:16 "The remainder of the Jews in the king's provinces gathered together and protected their lives, had rest from their enemies, and killed seventy-five thousands of their enemies; but they did not lay a hand on the plunder."

AGAIN, anachronism! In an era of back hoes and tractors, it does not take 7 months to burry 75K. Mass graves can be done overnight. In ancient times, such a task would take many months.

Ezekiel 39:18,19 "You shall eat the flesh of the mighty, Drink the blood of the princes of the earth, Of rams and lambs, Of goats and bulls, All of them fatlings of Bashan. You shall eat fat till you are full, And drink blood till you are drunk, At My sacrificial meal Which I am sacrificing for you."

This is prophetic language describing victory over Israel's persecutors. They saw God's judgment upon those who sought to have their blood. They were partaking of His vengeance upon their persecuting enemy's blood.

This is exactly what happened in Esther!

We see the same prophetic language in the book of Revelation.

Revelation 19:18 "that you may eat the flesh of kings, the flesh of captains, the flesh of mighty men, the flesh of horses and of those who sit on them, and the flesh of all people, free and slave, both small and great.""

In Revelation, God uses the beast (Rome) to judge the harlot, Israel (Revelation 17:16). The beast (Rome) that the harlot (Israel) was using, riding upon (17:7), to carry out the persecution against Christians, turned on the Harlot, Israel.

Revelation 17:16 "And the ten horns which you saw on THE BEAST, these shall HATE THE HARLOT, make her desolate and naked, eat her flesh and burn her with fire."

God turned things on Israel, as the new strategy of Rome was to destroy Israel, as they saw Christianity as but a sect of Judaism. General Titus said, "'The temple is distinguished above all human achievements. Its destruction will take care of the root and the offshoot ".

The root meaning Judaism and the offshoot Christianity.

They thought that Christians depended on the land and temple when Jesus was all of that to them. The natural mind still believes that the land and temple mean something to the heart, mind, and plan of God!

God's people saw this as His judgment upon their persecutors!

Ezekiel 39:20 "You shall be filled at My table With HORSES and riders, With mighty men And with all the men of war," says the Lord God."

Again, sensationalist "Bible Prophecy" writers, please stop HORSING AROUND!

The most evil generation in history, killing Jesus, His apostles, and a multitude of His disciples, received the severest of judgments. The judgements throughout the Old Testament are cited in the book of Revelation.

Luke 11:51 "from the blood of Abel to the blood of Zechariah, who was killed between the altar and the house of God; yes, I tell you, it shall be charged against this generation."

Again, Sodom, Egypt, Balaam, Babylon, and Jezebel are all cited in the book of Revelation. Noah is mentioned by Jesus in the Olivet Discourse concerning the same judgement coming upon that Generation in Matthew 24:37-41.

Blood five feet deep to the horses' bridles?

In these wars, Revelation 14: 20 says, "And the wine press was trampled outside the city, and blood came out from the wine press, up to the horses' bridles, for a distance of 1,600 stadia." That's about 184 miles long. Many futurists say that this is five feet deep in blood, stretching to nearly the entire length of the nation of Israel. I had my friend, who has a doctorate in Mathematics, and is a professor at ORU, run the numbers for 5 feet of blood just in the valley of Megiddo alone, which is something like 25 miles by 10 miles. He calculated the quarts of blood per person it would take to fill the valley. It would take about 22,000 times the world's present population! Figure in absorption and you could probably double that number! Futurism doesn't add up and is embarrassing!

The description of blood to the horse's bridal is hyperbolic and prophetic apocalyptic language.

The progression of such events is in the order of which Jesus describes, wars lead to economic collapse, which leads to famine, which causes starvation and death, leaving rotting corpses, which creates pestilence and disease. We see this progression in the next verse 24:7, which is also parallel with Revelation 6:4-8.

CHAPTER 11

EARTHQUAKES

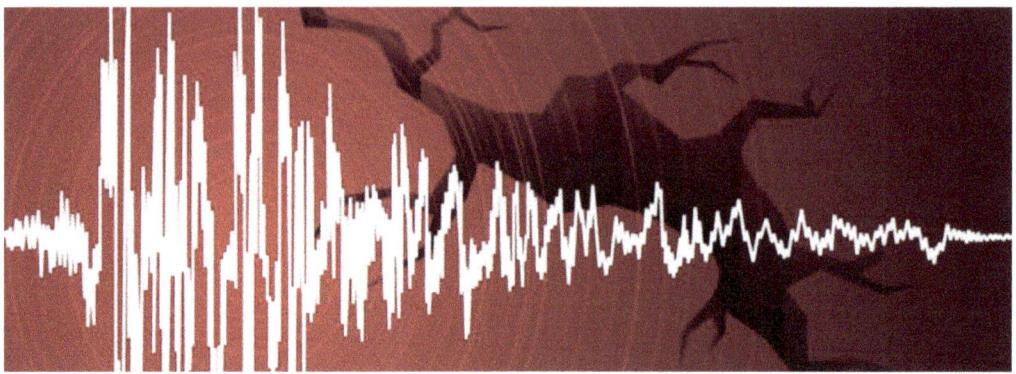

Matthew 24:7

"For nation shall rise against nation, and kingdom against kingdom: and there shall be famines, and pestilences, and earthquakes in various places."

Again, self-explanatory as this verse lays out the natural progression of war, causing famine, causing death and rotting corpses, creating pestilence and disease here. At the end of the verse, we see earthquakes.

I often hear dispensational teachers, the only ones on the airwaves and in popular churches, say that EARTHQUAKES and their devastations have increased in our day as opposed to days gone past. Here is a brief list of some earthquakes in history and their devastations.

Date AD: Location: Deaths:

532 Syria 130,000

678 Syria 170.00

856 Iran:Qumis Damghan 200,00

893 India: Daipul 180,00

893 Iran: Ardabil 150,000

1138 Egypt, Syria 230,000

1139 Iran: Gansana 100,000

1290 China: Chihili 100,000

556 China 830,000

1641 Iran: Dehkwargan, Tabriz 300,000

1662 China 300,000

1669 Sicily: (Etna eruption) 100,000

1693 Sicily: Catania and Naples 100,000

1703 Japans: Hokkaido 100,000

1721 Iran: Tabriz 100,000

1730 China:Chihili 100,000

1730 Japan: Hokkaido 137,000

1731 China: Peking 100,000

1737 India: Calcutta 300,000

1780 Iran: Tabriz 100,000

1850 China 300-400,000

1876 Bay of Bengal (tsunami) 215,000

1908 Italy: Messina/Reggio 110,000

Today there is an increase in technology so as to monitor earthquakes more precisely, not an increase in actual earthquakes.

From the time of Jesus death in the early 30's, to 70 A.D. (The span of a generation, about 40 yrs.), earthquakes did increase. Just prior to 70 A.D., there were earthquakes in Crete, Smyrna, Miletus, Chios, Samos, Laodicea, Hierapolis, Colosse, Campania, Rome, Judea, and Pompeii.

Henry Alford compiled this list leading up to 70 A.D., with the destruction of the temple, and of the city of Jerusalem.

1. A great earthquake in Crete, A.D. 46 or 47.
2. One at Rome on the day when Nero assumed the "manly toga." (To much info here Henry, spare us the details) A.D. 51.

3. One at Apamaea in Phrygia, mentioned by Tacitus, A.D. 53.

4. One at Laodicea in Phrygia, A.D. 60.

5. One in Campania. Seneca, in the year, A.D. 58, writes: "How often have cities of Asia and Achaea fallen with one fatal shock! So many cities have been swallowed up in Syria, how many in Macedonia! How often has Cyprus been wasted by this calamity! How often has Paphos become a ruin! News has often been brought us of the demolition of whole cities at once."

Flavius Josephus, the captured Jewish General, and Roman Historian, speaks of earthquakes within Israel at this time. He describes an earthquake in Judea, as follows, "that the constitution of the universe was confounded for the destruction of men." He expounds on this quake and writes that the Judean earthquake was "no common" calamity, indicating that God Himself had brought it about for a specific purpose.

CHAPTER 12

MATTHEW 24:8-13

PERSECUTION

Matthew 24:8-13 says,

"All these are the beginning of sorrows. Then shall they deliver YOU up to be afflicted, and shall kill YOU: and YOU SHALL BE HATED OF ALL NATIONS FOR MY NAMES SAKE... And then shall many be offended, and shall betray one another, and shall hate one another. And many false prophets (Acts 13:6) shall rise and shall deceive many. And because iniquity shall abound, the love of many shall wax cold. BUT HE THAT SHALL ENDURE UNTO THE END, THE SAME SHALL BE SAVED".

As we continue to interpret scripture with scripture, we see the exact thing being said in Matthew 10:16-23. The same betrayal and persecution to happen to Jesus' first century disciples. These two passages have to be speaking of the same thing. The words are in effect given to us verbatim, "AND YOU SHALL BE HATED OF ALL MEN FOR MY NAME'S SAKE, BUT HE THAT ENDURETH TO THE END SHALL BE SAVED."

Matthew 10:22. Again, these two passages of scripture cannot be separated from one another, unless one is wrongly dividing the word of truth (2 Timothy 2:15)!

And to throw a wrench into the dispensational delusion, the next verse in Matthew 10:23 says, "YOU shall not have gone over the cities of Israel, till the Son of man comes". Jesus said that He is coming in the first century here! Put that in your Dispensational pipe and smoke it!

This gospel did go over the cities of Israel and into all the world, as we read the next verse in the Olivet Discourse.

CHAPTER 13

MATTHEW 24:14

The Good News of the Kingdom Preached in all the Roman World (Oikoumene) As a Witness to all Nations.

Matthew 24:14,

"And this GOSPEL OF THE KINGDOM SHALL BE PREACHED IN ALL THE WORLD for a witness unto all nations; and then shall the end come."

The word for "world" here is "Oikoumene" in the Greek. It is defined as, "LAND, i.e. the (terrene part of the) globe; SPECIFICALLY, THE ROMAN EMPIRE: —earth, world. It is not at all referring to the globe, as such an idea wasn't even understood in that day. Consider its usage in Luke 2:1, "And it came to pass in those days, that there went out a decree from Cæsar Augustus, that ALL THE WORLD should be taxed." That tax/census went out only to the Roman World, not to the globe. It did NOT go out to North America, Australia or Japan.

The gospel did go out into all of the Roman world and turned it upside down, Acts 17:6 "…these are they that have turned the WORLD upside down", again, the "Oikoumene" Roman world.

Romans 10:18 says the same, "But I say, Have they not heard? Yes verily, Their sound went into all the earth, And their words unto the ends of the WORLD." The Roman world. "Oikoumene".

Colossians 1:5,6 says it again, "…THE GOSPEL, which has come to you, as it is IN ALL THE WORLD".

This word for world is "Kosmos", meaning the arrangement, not really the globe.

Colossians 1:23 makes it very clear, "the gospel that you have heard, which WAS proclaimed in all creation under heaven (Kosmos)".

Romans 1:8 communicates the same, "…your faith is spoken of THROUGHOUT THE WHOLE WORLD (Kosmos)."

Romans 16:25,26 speaks of the gospel going to all nations, "…my GOSPEL AND THE PREACHING OF JESUS CHRIST …but now is made manifest, and by the scriptures of the prophets, according to the commandment of the everlasting God, MADE KNOWN (Past tense) TO ALL NATIONS for the obedience of faith:"

THE APOSTLES did this with the fullness of Jesus' power, as we read in the great commission.

Matthew 28:18-20 Says, "And Jesus came and spake unto them, saying, All power is given unto me in heaven and in earth. Go ye therefore, and teach all nations, baptizing them in the name of the Father, and of the Son, and of the Holy Ghost: teaching them to observe all things whatsoever I have commanded you: and, lo, I am with you alway, even unto the end of the age. Amen."

JESUS HAS ALL POWER, AND HE SENDS THEM WITH THAT POWER! Is this something that's missed by evangelicals in thinking that the devil has the power to take over the earth with an imagined "Antichrist"? The gospel is the "power of God" (Romans 1:16). Is there some kind of power out there that is greater than "the power of God"? This is an offensive attack mode mandate to take the land! Notice that Jesus is talking about the gospel taking over NATIONS here! It is increasing His government (Isaiah 9:7)! It is not the gospel of our day, which talks about after you die, you'll go to heaven. That sounds like the gospel of death! It's about living people teaching living nations the truths of His word! Note, that Jesus did not say that the devil has the predetermined power to take over the world through an Antichrist, around which time I'm going to rapture you out of here (John 17:15)! Today we are given this evil report! "You can't claim the European nations for Christ and make disciples of them, because they're from where the antichrist takes over the world. Russia? No, they're end times bad guys. The Middle East? No, Iraq is this, and Iran is that end time bad guy. China? No, kings of the east..." Enough of your evil report, Misleaders!

Another convoluted evil report exists amongst mostly charismatic Christians, of whom I am one, is the belief that the world is prophesied to, and therefore predetermined to, become darker and darker, but the church will get brighter and brighter. This makes no rational sense whatsoever! If light increases, darkness lessens and is expelled by increased light. This is schizophrenic thinking that both light and darkness increase together!

I believe that the following quote from Charles Spurgeon was prophetic, concerning Revelation 11:15, which says, "Then the seventh angel sounded: And there were loud voices in heaven, saying, "The kingdoms of this world have become the kingdoms of our Lord and of His Christ, and He shall reign forever and ever!"

Here's Spurgeon's quote.

"It would be easy to show that at our present rate of progress the kingdoms of this world never could become the kingdom of our Lord and of His Christ. Indeed, MANY IN THE CHURCH ARE GIVING UP THE IDEA OF IT EXCEPT ON OCCASION OF THE ADVENT OF CHRIST, WHICH, AS IT CHIMES IN WITH OUR OWN IDLENESS, IS LIKELY TO BE A POPULAR DOCTRINE. I myself believe that King Jesus will reign, and the idols be utterly abolished; but I expect the same power which turned the world upside down once will still continue to do it. The Holy Ghost would never suffer the imputation to rest upon His holy name that He was not able to convert the world."

-Charles Spurgeon

The Great Commission in Matthew is concerned about making disciples of entire nations, not just to make individual believers as we see in Mark 16:15.

In Matthew we are to teach them all of Jesus' words. "Teaching them to observe all things that I have commanded you"

-Matthew 28:20

The Great Commission is not just about producing newborn believers, but teaching them and making disciples, disciplined ones (John 8:32)! You feed a baby healthy milk, then solid food (1 Corinthians 3:2, Hebrews 5:12-14), up to the meat of the word! In our day, babies are born, and they're fed the fast food, the junk food of Dispensationalism! It's a 2 for 1 deal. Believe in Jesus plus receive a darker and darker worldview, Israel is this and that part of the plan, we're about to do a disappearing act, an antichrist is about to take over the world, and everything is then going to be nuked! Because not a word of this teaching is true, this produces unhealthy children!

Again, the teaching emphasis of Jesus! In the gospels, He teaches, teaches and teaches, then confirms the teaching with a miracle. Teaching effects thinking, which leads to various actions or inactions.

True teaching was working with the prophetic in Acts 13:1, "Now in the church that was at Antioch there were certain prophets and teachers".

When teaching and prophetic work together, often they don't, four chapters later we read that they "turned the world upside down" (Acts 17:6).

If the prophetic works with the wrong teachers and teachings, such as dispensationalism today, you have the world turning the church upside down! I remember being very grieved about this when I saw all of the prophetic ministries operating under the falsehood of premillennialism. Peter Wagner encouraged me that he too saw the problem and was writing a book," Dominion" that addressed some of this. He was also talking about this with John Eckhardt, who saw these things clearly. John saw that premillennial dispensationalism was misleading many. I talked with John of how it seemed that Kim Clement had reverted back to dispensationalism, and he agreed. I Just found out lately that Kim had done exactly that and embraced Chuck Missler as his mentor on these matters. I believe that Kim was seduced and that God then took him home.

Psalm 2 is the second most quoted Old Testament passage quoted in the New Testament. It basically says, "Why do the nations rage and imagine a vain thing against the Lord and His anointed? He will laugh at them (This is powerful against evil rulers) and mock them and bring His wrathful word against them and terrify them!

God brought forth His Son, who would ask Him for the nations, which He does as we are in Him, and He in us! He takes possession of the very ends of the earth and breaks the nations with a rod of iron. He breaks the evil strongholds! He then warns the nation's to be wise.

The power of God topples the nations and turns them upside down (Acts 17:6)! He then warns the kings again to turn with affection to His Son, and receive His goodness, so that they don't partake of His wrath!"

I often hear how that it's going to be great someday in the by and by when a 5'6 (average first century height) Jesus in a robe comes and rules the nations with a rod of iron. Psalm 2 is quoted in Revelation 2:26,27, "And HE THAT OVERCOMES, and keepth my works unto the end, TO HIM WILL I GIVE POWER OVER THE NATIONS, AND HE SHALL RULE THEM WITH A ROD OF IRON. as the vessels of a potter shall they be broken to shivers: even as I received of my Father."

The Greek word for "rule" here is "poimaino". It means to tend as a shepherd, to feed, rule. The staff is used to direct the sheep away from danger, cliffs and wolves, etc... The feeding is the good word of God in its wisdom, love, power and truth. His word is the highest authority and prevails against all others. He, and we who are in Him, have the final word! What He, and we who are in Him, says goes! Speak His word in faith to leaders. Speak His word as a leader! As the missionaries spoke to the cultural practice in India, where they used to burn young wives alive on top of their older deceased husbands' bodies. They pled and reasoned against this practice, and it was stopped. Missionaries on the Amazon did the same toward a tribe that used to burry twin babies alive, thinking that such was a curse. The practice was stopped! Slavery was opposed by those speaking the word of God through William Wilberforce and many others. Lincoln quoted the scriptures more than any president as he led our nation to abolish slavery. The Civil Rights movement did exactly this in touching the conscience of a nation with the truth of the word of God! It was led by a preacher of the word, Martin Luther King. Reagan quoted the word nearly as much as Lincoln and brought down "The Evil Empire"! So today, the wisdom, truth and love of God comes through His word to those practicing abortion. Jesus is the life and brings life to the nations!

This is not a 5'6 Jesus ruling, but it is Jesus ruling through a first century church in Revelation 2:26,27, which is quoting Psalm 2.

Revelation 2:26,27 "And he that overcomes, and he that keeps unto the end my works, to him will I give authority over the nations, and he shall shepherd them with an iron rod; as vessels of pottery are they broken in pieces, as I also have received from my Father;"

This rule is promised under the condition that they overcome!

This is overcoming faith. "For whosoever is born of God overcomes the world: and this is THE VICTORY THAT OVERCOMES THE WORLD, EVEN OUR FAITH" (1 John 5:4)!

The church is waiting for the Jesus "in the days of His flesh" to do this (Hebrews 5:7), when Jesus is waiting for us to "'Ask it of Me, and I will certainly give the nations as Your inheritance, And the ends of the earth as Your possession" (Psalm 2:8).

Psalm 110 is the most quoted passage from the Old Testament in the New Testament. It says more or less the same thing as Psalm 2, "Jesus is sitting on the throne, making His enemies His footstool and then ruling in the midst of His enemies!

The people are then willing to submit to Him, because of the demonstration of His power! He then will judge the nations and their kings, severely! "We have such a weak position in approaching the nation and culture, when in reality we have all of the power of The Word Himself, who can outsmart the loudest of liars out there! This includes the Commie politicians to the hypocritical Hollywood actors (Gk. Hypokrites), which includes Provda journalists in our media! The book of Revelation has endless application, as the "false prophet" (Revelation 16:13, 19:20, 20:10) was the murderous smooth-talking Pharisees in the first century, and in our day, we can apply this to the murderous smooth-talking left, lying through the media! He is The Word and He will give us the words to shut them down! Luke 21:15 says, "for I will provide you utterance and wisdom which none of your opponents will be able to oppose or refute."

This is why evil antichrist systems hate free speech. Leftist Commies, Islam, and many in Israel know that The Truth, Jesus, The Word and The Spirit of Truth will defeat them! Leftist college students and protesters often follow their leaders' orders to not engage in dialogue with their opponents and will often use violence instead. They will not reason, because they are unreasonable people! Why are we paying for these universities, Maoist indoctrination camps, with our tax money! We can see the founding father's wisdom in prioritizing free speech as the very First Amendment!

Let us pray accordingly, "praying at the same time for us as well, that God will open up to us a door for the word, so that we may proclaim the mystery of Christ, for which I have also been imprisoned" (Colossians 4:3). This prayer was answered as Claudius Ceasar allowed free speech and the Good News turned the empire upside down!

The defeatist attitude, derived from Dispensational teaching says to retreat from the public square and hunker down until we "fly away, no glory", you know, the stupid church song!

The first century church laid the foundations for our faith. They are "THE GENERATIONAL" model for us, to quote my friend Terry Kashian.

Ephesians 2:20 says, "having been built on the foundation of the apostles and prophets, Christ Jesus Himself being the corner stone,"

Revelation 21:14 "And the wall of the city had TWELVE FOUNDATION STONES (1 Peter 2:5), and on them were the twelve names of the twelve apostles of the Lamb."

We are to go and do likewise! Every generation has the choice to do all, some, or none of His will!

Acts 13:22 says this, "After He had removed him, He raised up David to be their king, concerning whom He also testified and said, 'I have found David, the son of Jesse, a man after My heart, WHO WILL DO ALL MY WILL'"

They did it! They are the generational model! They "turned the world upside down" (Acts 17:6). Which was "the thousand-year reign"

CHAPTER 14

MATTHEW 24:14

Gospel of The Kingdom and the Thousand Year Reign and the Premillennial Cult.

For the vast majority of church history, most in our day do not know that premillennialism was considered a heresy.

Eusebius Pamphilius, (263-339 A.D.) Bishop of Caesarea in Palestine.

The following are excerpts from Eusebius' comments concerning the Writings of Papias, in Book 3, Chapter 39.

"This same historian (Papias) also gives other accounts, which he says he adds as received by him from unwritten tradition, likewise certain *strange parables of our Lord, and of His doctrine* and some other matters rather *to fabulous*. In these he says there would be *A CERTAIN MILLENNIUM* after the resurrection, and that there would be *a corporeal reign of Christ on this very earth*; *which things he appears to have imagined*, as if they were authorized by the apostolic narrations, *not understanding correctly* those matters which they propounded mystically in their representations. For he was very *limited in his comprehension*, as is evident from his discourses; yet he was the cause why *most of the ecclesiastical writers*, urging the antiquity of man, *were carried away by a similar opinion;* as, for instance, Irenaeus, or any other that adopted such sentiments."

Epiphanies, (315-403 A.D.) Early Church father states the following.

"There is indeed *A MILLENNIUM* by St. John; but the most, and those pious men, look upon those words as true indeed, but *to be taken in a spiritual sense*."

Isaiah 11:9 "They will not hurt or destroy in all My holy mountain, For the earth (land, nations) will be full of the knowledge of the Lord As the waters cover the sea", which is also in Habakkuk 2:14, and in Daniel 12:4, where this knowledge increases, which is not scientific knowledge, but the knowledge of the Lord! *"Of the INCREASE of His government there shall be no end"* (Isabiah 9:7). Turn off that Sci Fi channel and turn on the History channel!

The non hurting is in regard to the various animals at peace with one another in the previous verses, "the wolf shall dwell with the lamb" (Isaiah 11:6-8). These various animals are gentile people groups as we undeniably see in the next verse as it's quoted in the New Testament "(Isaiah 11:10/Romans 15:12).

Romans 15:12 quoting Isaiah 11:10 "And again, Isaiah says, There shall be a root of Jesse, And he that shall rise to **REIGN** over the Gentiles; In him shall the Gentiles trust."

Let me emphasize again, when does this happen? "AND IN THAT DAY, THERE SHALL BE A ROOT OF JESSE " (Isaiah 10:11). What day? Paul says it's in his day as he quotes Isaiah 10:11 in Romans 15:12, "And again, Isaiah says: "There shall be a ROOT OF JESSE; And He who shall rise to REIGN over the Gentiles, In Him the Gentiles shall hope."

This was the expansion of the kingdom to reach out and include the Gentiles.

This miraculous peace between these animals, really gentile people groups, is considered by all that I've heard to be the **THOUSAND YEAR REIGN** of Revelation 20. Isaiah 11:6 says that "the Wolf (Not the lion) shall dwell with the lamb". This is not a Mutual of Omaha kingdom being described here. Most Jehovah's Witnesses publications promote this carnal kingdom, as do many evangelicals. This is the exact word Paul uses, "REIGN" and He says that it's happening right now with the gospel of peace going out to the gentiles! It is the Kingdom of God's expansion to include them into "righteousness, peace, and Joy" in the Holy Spirit, which is the Kingdom of God (Romans 14:17). Note that Peter's vision is of various animals that represent the Gentiles in Acts 10.

The gospel is the "power of God" (Romans 1:16). It is this power that overcomes as we "BIND the strong man" and "plunder his goods" (Matthew 12:29)!

This is the binding of Satan!

Revelation 20:2 "He laid hold of the dragon, that serpent of old, who is the Devil and SATAN AND BOUND HIM for a thousand years;"

Remember that **"A THOUSAND"** is used throughout scripture and it is not meant to communicate mathematics. Also, note that Revelation 20 is the only mentioning of **"A THOUSAND YEAR REIGN"**. It is nowhere else in the book of Revelation, not in the epistles, the gospels, the psalms, the prophets, or in the law! Premillennialism builds its entire structure on this phrase in believing it to be mathematical. True apostolic teaching has at least 2 or 3 examples (witnesses) from other scriptures to confirm a matter. Is the chain binding Satan also literal, made of alloy or something to restrain a spirit being in Revelation 20:1,2? Scripture consistently uses "A THOUSAND" in a non-mathematical manner. Let's understand that the word literal is taken from the word literature. How does the rest of the literature, the Bible, use the phrase "A THOUSAND"?

Psalm 50:10 "For every beast of the forest is mine, And the cattle upon **A THOUSAND HILLS.**"

God owns the thousand and first hill as well as all the millions of hills in the world. Mathematics is not involved here!

Psalm 84:10 "For a day in thy courts Is better than **A THOUSAND** elsewhere".

A thousand and one, or two thousand days are not any better elsewhere either! Mathematics is not the point!

Think of the beautiful song, "A Thousand Years", by Christina Perri. It's a love song that one has in their heart for another. Such love mathematically is only going to be for a good 50-100 years maximum.

Job 9:3 "If one wished to dispute with Him, He could not answer Him once in **A THOUSAND.**"

Neither could one not answer and confound God, if they were given 2000 attempts to do so! I could give another thousand examples. But then I'd have to tell you that I've told you a thousand times that the inspired word of God is not being literal when using the words **"A THOUSAND**!

Deuteronomy 7:9 "Therefore know that the Lord your God, He is God, the faithful God who keeps covenant and mercy for **A THOUSAND** generations with those who love Him and keep His commandments"

Here is a real math problem for the literalist. A generation is 40 years, times a thousand means 40k years. Therefore, God is going to be keeping covenant for **A THOUSAND GENERATIONS** from the time this was written, so there's nearly 36K years before any so-called end of peoples.

What's more amazing is that the literal word for **"THOUSAND", is literally defined as being plural and nonliteral!**

χίλιοι chílioi, khil'-ee-oy; **PLURAL** of **UNCERTAIN** affinity; **A THOUSAND**:—thousand.

"I have loved you for a THOUSAND years, I'll love you for a THOUSAND more"

Another time indicator on "THE THOUSAND YEAR REIGN" is given to us in Matthew's gospel.

Matthew 19:28 "And Jesus said to them, "Truly I say to you, that you who have followed Me, in the **REGENERATION** (paliggenesia) when the Son of Man will sit on His glorious throne, you also shall sit upon twelve thrones, JUDGING the twelve tribes of Israel.

Commentaries that I've read say that this verse refers to the thousand-year reign.

The verse gives us the timing of this event, "in the regeneration". This word, paliggenesía, is used **only one other time in the New Testament**. By interpreting scripture with scripture, we can interpret the meaning as to when this occurs.

TITUS 3:5 "He saved us, not on the basis of deeds which we did in righteousness, but in accordance with His mercy, by the washing of **REGENERATION** (paliggenesia) and renewing by the Holy Spirit,"!

Paul says, by the Holy Spirit that the regeneration of Matthew 19:28 was occurring in his day! Therefore, Matthew 19:28's thousand-year reign is in Titus 3:5, in Paul's day!

I have much more written on this in "The Kingdom Bible", which is the thickest and heaviest Bible I've ever seen. And it weighs A TON! Not 2K pounds, but A FIGURATIVE TON!

We see clearly these same THRONES of Matthew 19:28 ruling and executing JUDGEMENT in Revelation 20, the millennium chapter!

Revelation 20:4 "And I saw THRONES, and they sat on them, and JUDGEMENT was committed to them. Then I saw the souls of those who had been beheaded for their witness to Jesus and for the word of God, who had not worshiped the beast or his image, and had not received his mark on their foreheads or on their hands. And they lived and reigned with Christ for a thousand years."

Another clear time indicator given to us for The Thousand Year Reign is in Revelation 1:1,3, 22:10. The prophecy of the book of Revelation, chapter 20 included, was something that "must SOON take place" (the very first verse), and it was "near/at hand"(1:3)! And the end of the book, "literally" says the same, "And he said to me, "Do not seal up the words of the prophecy of this book, for the time is near/at hand" (22:10). These are book ends to the vision of Revelation. And there is no way to stretch the definitions and New Testament usages of these timing words (Tachos, Engýs) to mean thousands of years later. Again (Phil.3:1), consider Ezekiel's prophecy in chapter 12, when God corrects the time that the prophecy was to occur. The people are falsely believing that the timing of the prophecy with the attitude that "The days are prolonged" (12:22), "The vision that he sees is for many days to come, and he prophesies of the times that are far off" (12:27). God corrects the timing misunderstanding by saying, "The days are at hand/near" (12:23), "it shall no more be prolonged/delayed, for in your days, O rebellious house, will I say the word, and will perform it…" (12:25), "none of my words will be prolonged any more, but the word I have spoken shall be done, says The Lord" (12:28). So "at hand/near" and "no more prolonged" can't mean thousands of years off, any more than, "far off, prolonged/delayed" can mean tomorrow! Words have to mean something!

When God says, "WITH THE LORD a day is as a thousand years, and a thousand years is as one day" (2 Peter 3:8), this is the perspective of God, who is outside of time! This is not talking about man's perspective of time! Why would God then communicate to man and say, "THE CAPTIVITY (70 years) IS LONG" (Jeremiah 29:28), if He was referring to His perspective of time? Is it long for God, or for man who is in time? Also note, in 2 Peter 3 here, that the "last days (of the old covenant age) mockers", where Old Testament Jews, believing their system would continue, "for ever since the fathers (Jewish fathers) fell asleep, all things continue as they were…" (2 Peter 3:3,4).

Timing is everything, and the book of Revelation has the prophetic time indicators of "soon", and "at hand/near" (1:1,3,22:10). Note that Revelation in 22:10, John is instructed to "SEAL NOT the sayings of the prophecy of this book, for the time is "AT HAND". Daniel is told to do the exact opposite in his book, which prophecies are talking about the same things, They are prophecies that are for nearly 600 years into the future. Daniel is told, "SEAL THE BOOK, even to the time of the end" (Daniel 12:4)! "Go your way, Daniel; for the words are SEALED UP until the time of the end" (not "end of time", but time of the end of the Old Covenant age). -Daniel 12:9

The prophecy/book was not for Daniel's day, "SEAL UP THE VISION, for it refers to many days in the future" (Daniel 8:26). Again, the timing words in these two prophetic books are exactly the opposite! "SEAL UP" and "SEAL NOT" (Daniel 12:4/Revelation 22:10) are prophetic time indicating words that have to mean something!

So the "THOUSAND YEAR REIGN" took place, when the Holy Spirit said it would, in John's Day (Rev.1:1,3,22:10, John 21:22).

Note that God is not a dumb thief! When He comes as a thief in 2 Peter 3:10 to bring the New Heavens and New Earth of Revelation 21, it is immediately AFTER the thousand-year reign in Revelation 20. A mathematical countdown removes any surprise of a thief coming! Another literalist implosion!

CHAPTER 15
MATTHEW 24:14

Gospel of the kingdom, Dominion over the BEASTS, including Mr. 666.

The Great Commission is a choice for each generation. It really began with the DOMINION MANDATE, first given to Adam, Genesis 1:26,"Then God said, "Let Us make man in Our image, according to Our likeness; and let them rule over the fish of the sea and over the birds of the sky and OVER THE BEASTS and over all the earth, and over every creeping thing that creeps on the earth."

Let's approach the scriptures in light of God's heart, mind and plan. Everything in the natural is a picture of something in the greater spiritual, first the natural, then the spiritual (1 Cor.15:46). So, when we read of animals and creeping things, what is the greater spiritual message? Consider, 1 Corinthians 9:9,10) "For it is written in the Law of Moses: "You shall not muzzle the ox while it is threshing." God is not concerned about oxen, is He? Or, is He speaking entirely for our sake? Yes, it was written for our sake, because the plowman ought to plow in hope, and the thresher to thresh in hope of sharing in the crops."

Physical fish are a type of men, as we are to be fishers of men (Matthew 4:19). The birds of the air are the principalities and powers in high places Ephesians 2:2, 6:12, 2 Corinthians 10:5).

Let's focus in detail here upon the **BEASTS** for a moment.

THE BEASTS are the fallen nature ruling through men. It's an illegitimate and ungodly evil rule. In Psalm 73:22, David recognizes his fallen nature after seeing things from God's perspective, "So foolish was I, and ignorant: I was as a BEAST before thee" (Psalm 73:22).

When Nebuchadnezzar was judged, he was reduced to his lowest state and told, "Your dwelling shall be with the beasts of the field" (Daniel 4:32). In Daniel 7, Daniel sees four "beasts" that were given dominion to rule.

"But the saints of the Highest One will receive the kingdom and take possession of the kingdom forever, for all ages to come"(Daniel 7:18).

Jesus takes dominion, ""And to Him was given dominion, Honor, and a kingdom, So that all the peoples, nations, and populations of all languages Might serve Him. His dominion is an everlasting dominion Which will not pass away; And His kingdom is one Which will not be destroyed" (Daniel 7:14).

The verse prior (7:13) is quoted by Jesus in Matthew 24:30, telling us that this was fulfilled in the first century, "This generation shall not pass, till all these things be fulfilled " (Matthew 24:34).

Jude 10 reveals that those outside of Christ are, "brute beasts", or "unreasoning animals" as the NASB puts it. The passage says that they are murderous like Cain. We say it today; he's acting like an animal! The lowest of lows in revealing man's fallen beast like nature is revealed in "the beast", who was the most powerful and exulted man in political history. He has "the number of a man (man, who was created on the 6th day, Gen.1:31) and his number is six hundred and sixty-six" (Rev.13:18). Did I mention that I changed my major to Political Science, because I was going to have the spiritual wisdom to decipher who Mr. 666 was in Europe to set up his "Antichrist" system to take over the world! Another strange fire to put out in futurist fiction prophecy books is the fact that the word "antichrist" is never used in the book of Revelation. It is only used in 1st and 2nd John.

Caesar Nero's name equates to exactly six hundred and sixty-six in the Hebrew letter numeric equation. This is what's known as Gematria and was a common practice amongst Jews. Each Hebrew letter has a number assigned to it. Neron Kesar or simply nrwn qsr, since Hebrew has no letters to represent vowels. It has been documented by archaeological finds that a first century Hebrew spelling of Nero's name provides us with precisely the value of 666. Jastrow's lexicon of the Talmud contains this very spelling." When we take the letters of Nero's name and spell them in Hebrew, we get the following numeric values: n=50, r=200, w=6, n=50, q=100, s=60, r=200 = 666.

Nero Caesar

נרונקסר

$$ר = 200$$
$$ס = 60$$
$$ק = 100$$
$$נ = 50$$
$$ו = 6$$
$$ר = 200$$
$$נ = 50$$

Sum: 666

It is the name and the title, Nero Caesar, to specify this political leader, that he is not some president or king in the distant future. He is a Roman Caesar. Think of the Holy Spirit's revelation of "Jesus Christ", the name and title, which equates 888 in its translation. Eight is the number of new beginnings in scripture.

Remember that the Jews said, we have no king but Caesar "(John 19:15). It Caesar that they chose over Jesus'. They rejected the "name above all other names" (Philippians 2:9)!

John 5:43 "I have come in My Father's name, and you do not receive Me; if another comes in his own name, him you will receive."

Remember that Christianity comes from Jewish peoples. The synagogues would often read in Hebrew, even though the empire primarily spoke Greek. Their influence was in every city throughout the empire, having synagogues in every city (Acts 15:21). The book of Revelation has so much Jewish appeal. Three fourths of its contents, 278 of 404 verses, are references or direct quotes from the Old Testament! One of the books most quoted from the Old Testament in Revelation is Ezekiel, who prophesied of Jerusalem's judgement by the Babylonians. The Old Testament bad guys, that would be judged, are throughout the book. Sodom, Egypt, Babylon, Magog, Balaam, Jezebel, as well as those who were delivered from such persecutors, Moses, Israel, the 12 tribes, David, and the prophets, are all mentioned in the book. The focus in the book is on Old Testament Jews, who were leading the persecution against New Testament believers. "The Great City" is Jerusalem (Rev.11:8/Luke 13:32). This is mentioned about a dozen times and is synonymous with "Babylon the Great". The Harlot (Isaiah 1:21) rides the corporate beast, Rome, in Revelation 17:7.

"And the angel said to me, "Why do you wonder? I will tell you the mystery of THE WOMAN AND OF THE BEAST THAT CARRIES HER, which has the seven heads and the ten horns."

If you're riding the beast, you have the reins and have complete control to make it go in whichever direction you wish!

Addressing Jews is the primary message of the entire book of Revelation, "Behold, I will make them of the synagogue of Satan, which say they are Jews, and are not, but do lie; behold, I will make them to come and worship before thy feet, and to know that I have loved thee." (Revelation 3:9)

Jewish influence over the Roman Empire is very under-appreciated! The Herod's were half Jewish. Most Jews read and wrote, when only 5% of the empire did! Nero's top advisor was Jewish. Jewish trade in the temple, for example, was off the charts profitable for all in the empire. All of the temple's goods are mentioned in Revelation 18, including "cattle" (18:11-13). Think about "cattle futures" alone! "The MERCHANTS of the land wept and mourned over her" (18:11), as they "saw the smoke of her burning" (18:9)!

Jesus exposed the Pharisees for running a house of MERCHANDISE (John 2:16)!

In light of this, consider Solomon exhibiting the fallen nature of man, joining with other gods of his wives. Solomon had fallen away and become apostate. He was committing spiritual immorality and unfaithfulness (Rev 2:22, 17:5/Isaiah 1:21, Rev 18:9,11,15). Solomon's gold weighed exactly 666 talents in 1 Kings 10:14.

Israel had gone the way of Solomon, as they joined with Rome. "We have no king but Caesar" (John 19:15). Israel was the clay (Isaiah 64:8, and they joined themselves to the iron, that was Rome (Daniel 2:33-35).

See the clear connection of these Pharisees to this chapter in Revelation, "And in her was found THE BLOOD OF PROPHETS, and of saints, and of ALL THAT WERE SLAIN UPON THE EARTH" (Revelation 18:24).

"…PROPHETS…YOU SHALL KILL…that upon you may come ALL THE RIGHTEOUS BLOOD SHED UPON THE EARTH, from the blood of righteous Abel unto the blood of Zacharias son of Barachias, whom ye slew between the temple and the altar" (Matthew 23:34,35).

The empire was not just made of iron, but of iron and clay (Daniel 2:41-43). Jews are referred to in scripture as the clay (Isaiah 64:8

Every Jewish reader, of course, saw that the Beast was a symbol of Nero.

Neron Caesar written in Hebrew characters (nrwn qsr) is equivalent to 666, whereas the Latin form of "Nero Caesar" (nrw qsr) is equivalent to 616."

This is why some Greek manuscripts have the number 616. This cannot be dismissed as those in a "crazy corner" as one futurist apologist argued. Note, that the top Greek scholar in the world, Bruce Metzger, is a primary proponent of this understanding, that is, that 616 was purposely written in many manuscripts, because it is the total of the Latin letter number equation.

Note that Nero was the 6th Roman Emperor, fittingly.

Revelation 17:10 "And there are seven kings: five are fallen, and one is, and the other is not yet come; and when he cometh, he must continue a short space."

Julius Caesar (49–44 BC), Augustus (27 BC–AD 14), Tiberius (AD 14–37), Gaius (AD 37–41), Claudius (AD 41–54), And "One is…" Nero (AD 54–68)", the sixth. "he must continue a short space", which is Galba (June AD 68–January AD 69. Galba reigned for about 7 months.

Remember that man, with Adam's fallen nature, was created the 6ᵗʰ day (Gen.1:31).

First century Christian's were given the Holy Spirit inspired word with the book of Revelation, which was addressed TO them (Rev.1:4). The book was written TO them, and FOR us. Consider this understanding in 1 Corinthians 10:11, "Now all these things happened to them as examples, and they were written FOR our admonition, upon whom the ends of the ages have come."

These Christians were implored to apply understanding in order to obtain the wisdom so as to determine the number of the beast (Rev.13:18)! Why would the Holy Spirit exhort them to apply understanding and obtain the wisdom as to who the man was, through the number of six hundred and sixty six, if it was for someone that was not on the scene in their day, but someone two thousand years later to be figured out by someone on line playing pin the tail on the beast? They were suffering the world's worst concentrated persecution of Christians, at which time God asked them to apply understanding to gain wisdom as to who this man was through the number six hundred and sixty-six, who was actually not going to be around for another couple thousand years! Preposterous! What kind of cruelty would such instructions be to benefit them as they were being fed to lions!

Nero was the epitome of the fallen beast nature of man. As he was the king at the top of the most brutal empire in history, he exhibited the lowest and worst of man's nature!

He had his mother Agrippina killed. He later killed his pregnant wife by kicking her in the stomach to kill the baby, which killed her as well. It is suspected that Agrippina had Claudius Caesar poisoned in order to have her son appointed Caesar. Nero was only 16 when he ascended to the throne.

"The beast", was what Nero's political opponents would refer to him as. He would dress himself in animal skins with his husband and bite off the genitals of Christian prisoners. He literally dressed up as a beast!

"No Christian pen can paint that revelry of Antichrist, or do more than distantly allude to the scenes which followed, when Nero, disguised in the skin of a bear, crawled on all fours among the vilest of those wretches, and gave to him 'who saw the Apocalypse' the image of the wild who sprang from the foul scum of the world's most turbid sea."

-FW Farrar (1831-1903)

Nero's palace had many images of half man; half beast creatures painted on its walls.

Nero would layer Christians in flammable oils and then coat them with wax to make them human candles, which made the burning process take much longer. The smell of such was enjoyed by Nero and Roman elites at the emperor's garden parties.

The fallen beast nature was on full display for all to see the depths of its shame in The Beast, Caesar Nero!

Nero demanded worship in making it the law to profess, "Caesar is Lord" before any purchase. Christians rebelled in saying, "Jesus is Lord". Therefore, they could not participate in buying and selling in the marketplace. The mark was a mark of ownership (Rev.13:16-18), as the very next verse refers to "The Lamb" and "His name and the name of His father written on their foreheads" (Rev.14:1). It's not written on their foreheads with a Sharpie! It's a matter of who you belong to, the Lamb or the beast? We even say today when perceiving something about someone, "it's written all over your face".

Numbers 6:25 "The Lord make His face shine on you, And be gracious to you;"

Caesar Nero erected a 120-foot statue of himself in the courtyard of his "Golden House".

As we understand that the individual beast was Nero, it's important to realize that the corporate beast was Rome. This was the Sea Beast, as the sea is referring to gentile nations (Genesis 10:5, Ps.72: 10, Is. 11:10, 11, 24:14-16, 65:5), across the seas, as opposed to people of the land, the promised land.

The application of this beast state worship is very appropriate in today's world! Think of recent history of some ruthless beast like governments, ruling with the desperately wicked and animalistic heart (Jeremiah 19:9) of the fallen nature. They literally demand worship, as we saw the people bowing down to Hirohito. Communism operates with the state being "God", and you cannot survive by not depending on them, or by disobeying them! They will see to that! "The government will provide all your need, according to their riches and glory", the beastly perversion of

Philippians 4:19! How many Christians in our country bow down to this government god to partake of its riches! They even have a demonic blood sacrifice offering through abortion! Many "Christians" have no problem with this! Get a conscience!

Let us remember that the Beast prophecy of the book of Revelation was to occur "quickly", "shortly", and it was "at hand/near" (Revelation 1:1,3,22:10). These Greek words, "Tachos" and "Engys" can never be made to stretch out for thousands of years, or to mean that that once the events start, then they will suddenly take place. Their literal definitions and New Testament usages forbid such distortions of men! This same time indicating, "engys" (near), used at the beginning of Revelation and at the end (Revelation 1:3, 22:10) is also found in Hebrews 8:13, "In that he saith, A new covenant, he hath made the first old. Now that which decayeth and waxeth old is READY TO VANISH AWAY (engys). The old covenant system had not passed when Hebrews was written in the 60's. It was still around and kicking. In AD 70, the temple and its old covenant system passed. The same use of this timing word is when Revelation 1:3 (Engys, "at hand/near"), written in the 60's, prophesies of the AD 70 events.

Timing is everything! If the Holy Spirit wanted to say that these events were literally at hand/near and soon to take place (Rev.1:1,3,22:10), what other words would He have used? If Jesus literally meant that the prophecy would be fulfilled in His generation, what other words would He have used to say this? Look again at Matthew 24:34, 16:28.

Do read "Before Jerusalem Fell", by Kenneth Gentry, and the points made by Robert Young, Isaac Newton, John Lightfoot, John Wesley, Jonathan Edwards, Phillip Schaff, Adam Clark, RC Sproul and many others concerning the early date of Revelation, as well as the Syriac Version of the Bible saying the following, "THE REVELATION WHICH WAS MADE UNTO JUHANON THE EVANGELIST, FROM ALOHA, IN PATHAMON THE ISLAND, WHITHER HE HAD BEEN CAST BY NERO CAESAR." Nero committed suicide in AD 68, therefore the book of Revelation was written prior to this.

Again, consider the prophecy in Ezekiel 12, where God says that its fulfillment is "at hand/near", that it's not "far off", "prolonged", as the people are saying, that it's "not in our day". They are corrected in their understanding of the timing of the prophecy. Therefore, "at hand/near" can't mean thousands of years off, anymore that "far off" and "prolonged" can mean tomorrow! Words do have to mean something!

We see the same timeline as the book of Revelation with "shortly", "quickly", and "at hand/near" (Rev.1:1,3,22:10) in the Olivet Discourse, which says, "This generation shall not pass, till all these things be fulfilled" (Matthew 24:34)!

Oh, that the church would come out of imagination with fiction "prophecy" books and into true revelation, particularly with the book of Revelation!

The great commission is the dominion mandate.

Genesis 1:26 "…let them have dominion over the fish of the sea (fishers of men, Mt.4:19), and over the fowl of the air (prince of the power of the air, Ephesians 2:2), and over the beasts (evil rulers, Daniel 7), and over all the earth (Peoples), and over every creeping thing that creepeth upon the earth."

The creeping things are the demonic and Satan himself, who is to be crushed underfoot (Gen. 3:15, Luke 10:19, Romans 16:20, Matthew 27:33).

Dominion was exercised over the beast by the church.

Revelation 15:2 "And I saw something like a sea of glass mixed with fire, and THOSE WHO WERE VICTORIOUS OVER THE BEAST and his image and the number of his name, standing on the sea of glass, holding harps of God."

ABRAHAM was given the DOMINION MANDATE, "as far as your eye can see " in Genesis 13:14,15, "The Lord said to Abram, after Lot had separated from him, "Now lift up your eyes and look from the place where you are, northward and southward and eastward and westward; for ALL THE LAND WHICH YOU SEE, I WILL GIVE TO YOU and to your descendants forever."

JOSHUA was given the DOMINION MANDATE, "Wherever your foot shall tread"!

Joshua 1:2-9, "Moses My servant is dead; now therefore arise, cross this Jordan, you and all this people, to the land which I am giving to them, to the sons of Israel. Every place on which the sole of your foot treads, I have given it to you, just as I spoke to Moses. From the wilderness and this Lebanon, even as far as the great river, the river Euphrates, all the land of the Hittites, and as far as the Great Sea toward the setting of the sun will be your territory. No man will be able to stand before you all the days of your life. Just as I have been with Moses, I will be with you; I will not fail you or forsake you. Be strong and courageous, for you shall give this people possession of the land which I swore to their fathers to give them. Only be strong and very courageous; be careful to do according to all the law which Moses My servant commanded you; do not turn from it to the right or to the left, so that you may have success wherever you go. This book of the law shall not depart from your mouth, but you shall meditate on it day and night, so that you may be careful to do according to all that is written in it; for then you will make your way prosperous, and then you will have success. Have I not commanded you? Be strong and courageous! Do not tremble or be dismayed, for the Lord your God is with you wherever you go."

This is the DOMINION MANDATE that is the model played out for us throughout scripture.

We don't need to get on an airplane to start from Jerusalem, then to Judea, to Samaria, to the uttermost parts of the earth (Acts 1:8). We are the uttermost parts of the earth from physical Jerusalem. The first century gives us this model, as they did His will in their generation (Acts 17:6, Romans 1:8,10:18,16:25,26, Colossians 1:5,6,23). We are to go and do likewise in our day and apply this to our location and sphere of influence. From our Jerusalem, Judea, Samaria, to the uttermost parts of the world, if you will. He was with them till the turbulent end of the old covenant age (Matthew 28:18-20), and He was still with them afterwards. He will be with us as we fulfill the dominion mandate in our day, regardless of the difficulties in various locations at various times. We have a generational model given to us by the apostles and prophets, the foundations of our faith (Ephesians 2:20, Revelation 21:14)!

THE GREAT COMMISSION IS THE DOMINION MANDATE!

Matthew 28:18-20 Says, "And Jesus came and spake unto them, saying, All power is given unto me in heaven and in earth. Go ye therefore, and teach all nations, baptizing them in the name of the Father, and of the Son, and of the Holy Ghost: teaching them to observe all things whatsoever I have commanded you: and, lo, I am with you always, even unto the end of the age. Amen." Remember Psalm 2/Revelation 2:26,27. We are to rule with a rod of iron. We start in OUR Jerusalem, Judea, Samariah, to the uttermost parts of the earth" (Acts 1:8)!

This gospel of the kingdom consumed the "world"! The word of God was like fire and the people like wood.

Jeremiah 5:14 "Wherefore thus saith the LORD God of hosts, Because ye speak this word, behold, I will make my words in thy mouth fire, and this people wood, and it shall devour them."

CHAPTER 16

MATTHEW 24:14

The Gospel of the Kingdom and the TWO WITNESSES.

In Revelation 11:5

"And if anyone wants to harm them, fire proceeds from their mouth and devours their enemies."

Jeremiah 5:14

"I will make My words in your mouth fire, And this people wood, And it shall devour them."

The word of God is the law and the prophets (Two Witnesses), preached by the apostles and prophets (Two Witnesses). Again, these TWO WITNESSES (Revelation 11:3), the "apostles and prophets" (Ephesians 2:20), were on the seen when the Holy Spirit said they would be," shortly" and "quickly" as the time was at "hand/near" (Rev.1:1,3,22:20).

They were persecuted unto the death in "THE GREAT CITY…. where our Lord was crucified" (Revelation 11:8). What city was our Lord crucified in?

Luke 13:33 "for it cannot be that a prophet should perish outside of JERUSALEM."

Location, location, location!

The preachers of the gospel were martyred, perhaps a broken 7 (completeness) is what 3 ½ days is referring to as their lives were cut short of completion. It looked like things were over, but they were replenished as God rose up new ones! Just as the death of Jesus made it look, but God resurrects!

Revelation 11:9 "Then those from the peoples, tribes, tongues, and nations will see their dead bodies three-and-a-half days and not allow their dead bodies to be put into graves."

Remember that Jerusalem was an international city. "And there were dwelling in Jerusalem Jews, devout men, from every nation under heaven." (Acts 2:5). Therefore, this verse is not talking about satellite television. Turn off the Sci-Fi channel and turn on the History Channel!

The two witnesses were the Apostles and Prophets (Ephesians 2:20) proclaiming the law and the prophets, the word of God, to the peoples!

Two witnesses, following God's principle.

2 Corinthians 13:1 "In the mouth of TWO or three WITNESSES shall every word be established."

Luke 10:1 "After these things the Lord appointed seventy others also and sent them TWO BY TWO before His face into every city and place where He Himself was about to go."

If these two witnesses were individuals, as James Stuart Russell believes they were, then Peter and James would fit the bill. James with the Moses teaching ministry and Peter with the Elijah power ministry. No written records of such would exist, as virtually the entire populous of the city was eliminated by the Roman armies. Also, Peter's death would be contrary to martyrdom in Rome, which some chalk up to as Catholic fiction anyway.

Either way, the Holy Spirit tells us when the Two Witnesses were to do their thing, "shortly" and the time was "at hand/near"! (Revelation 1:1,3,22:10).

Dominion has been the mandate since the beginning.

Sodom was visited by two witnesses, the two angels, that pronounced judgment upon it.

Egypt was confronted with the TWO WITNESSES of Moses and Aaron, who gave the Word of the Lord to Pharaoh and brought the most powerful nation in the world down for all the world to see, as His covenant people were victorious over them!

Assyria was then the most powerful nation, and the word of the Lord came through Jonah to the king, who was ruling from Nineveh. The entire nation turned to faith in relationship with the one true God! The word of the Lord came to Balaam from the mouth of a donkey. The whale or giant fish delivered the word of the Lord to the Assyria, Jonah, on their beach, two witnesses, haha?

Israel was briefly raised up as the "Son of David" built the temple, and all of Israel's enemies were put down as the land was subdued (Gen:1:26)

David and Solomon, two witnesses?

1 Chronicles 22:17,18 "David also commanded all the leaders of Israel to help his son Solomon, saying, "Is the Lord your God not with you? And has He not given you rest on every side? For He has handed over to me the inhabitants of the land, and the land is subdued before the Lord and before His people."

Note that the land of Israel was initially taken by TWO WITNESSES, Joshua and Caleb.

Babylon was the most glorious of kingdoms, a world governing empire. They heard the word of the Lord through Daniel, and Nebuchadnezzar was converted and proclaimed the truth of the one true God to the entire world over which he governed in Daniel 4. Nebuchadnezzar was a type, in his positives, of Jesus, the head of gold. Gold was the most valuable of the metals of Daniel's great image. Jesus is the head of the body of Christ. Even the parable of the kingdom with the birds in the tree, allude to Nebuchadnezzar as the type and Jesus' as the reality (Daniel 4:10-12, Matthew 13:32,33). Daniel and Ezekiel were two witnesses proclaiming the word of the Lord concerning Babylon.

Medo-Persia was also visited by God through the word given by Daniel and Esther, TWO WITNESSES, and Darius/ Ahasueres received that word and loved the messengers and believed in the one true God, Also, we see Esther and Mordecai were two witnesses in the king's palace.

Greece received much of the wisdom of God, through the word of the Lord given by the Jewish Rabbis. The Greek philosophers were astonished at their wisdom and sat at their feet in awe! The Jewish priests and rabbis, two witnesses.

And Josephus speaks of Alexander the Great being greatly influenced by the Jews.

He said that Alexander advanced toward Jerusalem after his victories over the Persian Empire, the High Priest Jaddua became anxious because the Jews had previously pledged their loyalty to Darius, the Persian king. Fearing Alexander's wrath, Jaddua prayed to God and received a vision during the night assuring him of divine protection. Based on this divine message, Jaddua dressed in his high priestly garments and, along with the priests and people clothed in white, went out of the city to meet Alexander in peace.

When Alexander saw the High Priest and the procession, he dismounted and bowed before the High Priest. His generals, especially Parmenio, were surprised by this act and asked him why he would show such reverence to the Jewish High Priest. Alexander replied that he did not bow to the man but to the God who had honored him with the priesthood. He explained that while still in Macedonia, he had seen a vision of this very priest in the same garments, encouraging him in a dream to cross into Asia and promising him victory over the Persians. Recognizing the priest from the vision, Alexander saw this moment as divinely appointed.

Alexander then entered Jerusalem peacefully. He was shown the Book of Daniel by the priests, where they interpreted a prophecy that they believed foresaw Alexander's rise and conquest of Persia. Pleased with this, Alexander granted favorable terms to the Jews, allowed them to keep their laws, and even promised that Jews in his realm could live according to their customs.

-Flavius Josephus, Antiquities of the Jews, Book 11, Chapter 8, Sections 4–5.

(William Whiston translation)

The Roman Empire saw the Stone cut out with hands (Daniel 2:34), Jesus' kingdom hit it. The entire Roman world was thereby turned upside down (Romans 1:8, 10:18, 16:25,26, Acts 17:6, Colossians 1:5,6,23)! Caesar's palace had literally been permeated with the word of the Lord (Philippians 1:13)! And we know that the apostle Paul delivered the death nail to Nero in preaching the word of the Lord to this demented being. Twice, he was brought before Nero. The Apostles and prophets were the TWO WITNESSES to the Roman Empire (Ephesians 2:20).

Note that the sovereign hand of God prepared and used the Roman roads to reach the ends of the Roman World! Advancements and technologies are tools that God uses to spread His word! The old nature believes the evil report that such things are created to allow the beast to carry out persecution! I was taught that computers and scanners were tools for The Antichrist to take over the world. Such an evil report (Numbers 13)!

CHAPTER 17

MATTHEW 24:15,16

THE ABOMINATION OF DESOLATION

Matthew 24:15,16

"When YOU (NOT THEY) therefore shall see the ABOMINATION OF DESOLATION, spoken of by Daniel the prophet, stand in the holy place, (whoso readeth, let him understand:) THEN LET THEM WHICH BE IN JUDAEA FLEE TO THE MOUNTAINS".

So many imaginations of men have been expressed in this, instead of the pure revelation of scripture, allowing for it to interpret itself! To start with, Jesus is prophesying of a future event and is not referring to something that occurred in the past with Antiochus Epiphanies.

The parallel verse for us is found in Luke 21:20,21 "And when ye shall see Jerusalem surrounded with armies, then know that the desolation thereof is nigh. THEN LET THEM WHICH ARE IN JUDAEA FLEE TO THE MOUNTAINS; and let them which are in the midst of it depart out; and let not them that are in the countries enter thereinto."

The exact same words are used, verbatim, therefore they are talking about the same thing. To divide them is to wrongly divide the word, which division is so often done on this subject matter, separating sister verses!

WHAT ARE THEY FLEEING?

Matthew 24:15,26 says it's

"THE ABOMINATION OF DESOLATION" and Luke 21:20,21 says "JERUSALEM SURROUNDED BY ARMIES", then know that the DESOLATION thereof is near".

It cannot be any clearer than seeing the ABOMINATION OF DESOLATION in Mt.24:15 is also defined as JERUSALEM SURROUNDED BY ARMIES, and it's DESOLATION in Luke 21:20! The same word "DESOLATION" is used in both passages and the same instructions are given in both after they "SEE" it, "FLEE" in the very next verse in both!

Jesus is referring to Daniel 9:27, which we've gone over, which no one ever taught was in our future until the Dispensational delusion began doing in the last hundred years or so! This abomination is also mentioned in Daniel 12:11.

"And he shall confirm the covenant with many for one week: and in the midst of the week he shall cause the sacrifice and the oblation to cease, and for the overspreading of ABOMINATIONS he shall make it DESOLATE, even until the consummation, and that DETERMINED shall be poured upon the desolate."

CLEARLY THE DESTRUCTION OF THE CITY AND TEMPLE IN AD 70!

It was "determined" and declared by Jesus within the 70 weeks that judgment/desolation was coming upon the city and sanctuary in His prophecy on the Mount of Olives (Mt.24, Mk.13, Lk.21), "The Olivet Discourse".

As for "standing in the holy place, where it ought not", that is, the Gentile Roman armies are the "it" here. Their trespassing onto the holy land, city and temple of the old covenant, which was an abomination, something abhorrent and detestable (the definition of abomination) to a Jew in the first century.

It is often taught, in our day, that this abomination of desolation is what we read of in 2 Thessalonians 2. The timing of these happenings can be connected, as well as it referring to the same event, in general. However, the details given to us in 2 Thessalonians 2:3-9 are very distinct in describing the various players.

3"Let no one deceive you by any means; for that Day will not come unless the falling away comes first, and the man of sin is revealed, the son of perdition, 4 who opposes and exalts himself above every so-called god or object of worship, so that he takes his seat in the temple of God, displaying himself as being God. 5 Do you not remember that while I was still with you, I was telling you these things? 6 And you know what restrains him now, so that in his time he will be revealed. 7 For the mystery of lawlessness is already at work; only he who now restrains will do so until he is taken out of the way. 8 Then that lawless one will be revealed, whom the Lord will slay with the breath of His mouth and bring to an end by the appearance of His coming; 9 that is, the one whose coming is in accord with the activity of Satan, with all power and signs and false wonders."

To start out, let's do away with the ridiculous notion that after a rapture in our future, the omnipresent Holy Spirit is the restrainer in verse 6 and will be removed from the earth, as millions are being evangelized without the work of the Holy Spirit!

Also, the belief that the man of sin is a Roman authority, such as Nero, committing the Abomination of Desolation is impossible. Again, these two passages (Mt.24:15,16 and 2 Thes.2) do not speak in detail of the same event. Christians are exhorted to flee the city when they see the Roman armies surrounding it (Luke 21:20,21). The Romans have not yet entered it as they surround it. Christians are to flee AFTER they SEE the abomination of desolation, "Therefore, when YOU SEE the abomination of desolation...FLEE (Mt.24:15,16). History records (Eusebius) that the Roman armies allowed, whosoever will, to leave the city before they entered it.

Now let's understand that the "seat" in the temple (vs 4) is not a physical seat, but it's talking about a position of authority (Mt.23:2, 27:19, John 19:13, Acts 18:12, 16,17, 25:6,10,17, Romans 14:10, 2 Cor. 5:10, Rev.2:13, 13:2, 16:10). We've ruled out that it could be referring to a Roman authority. Therefore, it was Jewish Authority committing this deed as they continued to offer animal sacrifices in the temple after the ultimate sacrifice of God's son had been made! The Jewish zealots had taken over the temple after killing the priests and leaving their blood to cover the temple's floor. The primary leader of the zealots was one John Levi of Gischala. Leading the people, the "sons of disobedience" (Ephesians 2:2, Colossians 3:6) in rejecting God's sacrifice, he took the place of God himself in the temple! The "sons of disobedience" (corporate) coincides with the "son of destruction" (individual). The same exact word is used in the passages (Eph.2:2, Col.3:6, 2 Thes.2:3), "Huios", Strongs G5207. This son was a people group, in reality, the sons of disobedience and destruction! The primary temple where this sitting in the temple and showing himself that he is God (2 Thes.2:4) was a heart thing. The word for temple here is "holy Naos", which can be used to describe the place of worship within the heart.

Here is a shortened version of the Vine's definition of "Naos": By Christ metaphorically, of His own physical body, John 2:19, 21. In Apostolic teaching, metaphorically of The Church, the mystical body of Christ, Eph.2:21; (2) of a local Church, 1 Cor.3:16, 17:2, 2 Cor.

6:16; (3) of the present body of the individual believer, 1 Cor. 6:19. If this last definition is what Paul is referring to, then it could be the edict of the Roman Emperor requiring all citizens to hail Caesar as Lord. This would then be referring to the worshipping the beast within, from the allegiance of an individual's heart/temple, which was intended for the worship of God alone. State worship was required for all transactions (Rev.13:17). "Caesar is Lord" was rejected by Christians who rebelled and said "Jesus is Lord"!

We see this in those who have "fallen away" in the passage (2 Thes.2:3). How does one fall away?

Hebrews 6:6 "and then have FALLEN AWAY, to restore them again to repentance, since they again crucify to themselves the Son of God and put Him to open shame"

They fall away by rejecting the sacrifice of Jesus and by returning to animal sacrifices! They returned to the old covenant law, "You have been severed from Christ, you who are seeking to be justified by the Law; you have FALLEN FROM GRACE."

(Galatians 5:4). This apostasy of the last days is also seen in Timothy.

1 Timothy 4:1-6 "Now the Spirit expressly says that IN LATTER TIMES some will depart from the faith, giving heed to deceiving spirits and doctrines of demons, speaking lies in hypocrisy, having their own conscience seared with a hot iron, forbidding to marry, and commanding to abstain from foods which God created to be received with thanksgiving by those who believe and know the truth. For every creature of God is good, and nothing is to be refused if it is received with thanksgiving; for it is sanctified by the word of God and prayer. IF YOU INSTRUCT THE BRETHREN IN THESE THINGS, you will be a good minister of Jesus Christ, nourished in the words of faith and of the good doctrine which you have carefully followed."

We see clearly that they are going back to the mosaic dietary laws.

Timothy is exhorted to counter these false teachings and bring correction, "IF YOU INSTRUCT THE BRETHREN IN THESE THINGS" (vs.6) He is not told by the Holy Spirit, through Paul, that these things would occur thousands of years later! They were happening in

Timothy's Day, in the last days of the Old Covenant age (Matthew 24:3,34, Acts 2:16-21, Hebrews 1:2)!

The same is seen in 2 Timothy.

2 Timothy 3:1-10 "But know this, that IN THE LAST DAYS perilous times will come: For men will be lovers of themselves, lovers of money, boasters, proud, blasphemers, disobedient to parents, unthankful, unholy, unloving, unforgiving, slanderers, without self-control, brutal, despisers of good, traitors, headstrong, haughty, lovers of pleasure rather than lovers of God, having a form of godliness but denying its power. And from such people turn away! For of this sort are those who creep into households and make captives of gullible women loaded down with sins, led away by various lusts, always learning and never able to come to the knowledge of the truth. Now as Jannes and Jambres resisted Moses, so do these also resist the truth: men of corrupt minds, disapproved concerning the faith; but they will progress no further, for their folly will be manifest to all, as theirs also was. BUT YOU have carefully followed my doctrine, manner of life, purpose, faith, longsuffering, love, perseverance,"

Timothy is exhorted to follow the true doctrine and counter these ways of the works of the flesh! The Holy Spirit is not saying that these works were going to occur in men some thousands of years later! Of course, flesh is flesh, and the old nature will always produce these works to be overcome by the Spirit (Galatians 5:19-23).

Luke 18:8 "I tell you that He will avenge them speedily. Nevertheless, when the Son of Man comes, will He really find faith on the EARTH (Gk. "Ge", as in geography, land)?"

The falling away is what Jesus is addressing here. It was the easy out to avoid persecution by leaving the faith and returning to the Old Covenant practices.

So, who was playing the role of RESTRAINING (2 Thes.2:6) these Zealots? It was Rome that kept the zealots in check. The zealots sought to liberate the nation through the sword. Once the 5-month siege (April-September AD 70, Rev.9:5) had begun from without, the zealots would take over from within.

And finally, futurism implodes with this verse as those who flee Judea and go to the mountains are spared from the judgment in Mt.24:15/Luke 21:20. If the judgment of the Olivet discourse (Mt.24, Mk.13, Lk.21), which is the same prophecy as the book of Revelation, is a global conflagration, what good is fleeing to the mountains going to do in an era of F-35's and Hydrogen Bombs?

So, Jerusalem is surrounded by armies (Matthew 24:15/Luke 21:20). It is the theme of the Olivet discourse prophecy! "O Jerusalem, Jerusalem, thou that killest the prophets, and stonest them which are sent unto thee, how often would I have gathered thy children together, even as a hen gathereth her chickens under her wings, and ye would not" (Matthew 23:37).

The book of Revelation is speaking of the same destruction of Jerusalem, "THE GREAT CITY…where also our Lord was crucified" (Revelation 11:8).

Where was our Lord crucified?

Luke 13:33 …for it cannot be that a prophet perish outside of Jerusalem."

To identify **"THE GREAT CITY",** is to identify Babylon/**The Harlot! This harlot rides the Beast, that is Rome**. (17:7,9) To ride a beast, one is in complete control, so as to direct it's every move. This point can't be made any clearer. With the exception of perhaps the timing verses, this is the single greatest key to **understanding the sayings of this book**. (1:3)

I will ask again, what city was our Lord **crucified in?** It's clearly **JERUSALEM** (Mt.16:21, Lk.13:33, Is.1:1,10 "Sodom"), **"THE GREAT CITY." Revelation 11:8** Therefore, the Great City/Babylon/The Harlot is Jerusalem.

Revelation 11:8 "…THE GREAT CITY, which spiritually is called Sodom and Egypt, where also our Lord was crucified." (That is, Jerusalem)

Revelation 14:8 "BABYLON is fallen, is fallen**, THAT GREAT CITY."**

Revelation 16:19 "THE GREAT CITY…and **GREAT BABYLON came** in remembrance…"

Revelation 17:1 "THE GREAT WHORE that sitteth upon many waters. (17:15)

Revelation 17:5 "…BABYLON THE GREAT, the mother of **HARLOTS."**

Revelation 17:18 "the woman/**HARLOT,** which thou sawest is **THAT GREAT CITY,"**

Revelation 18:2 "BABYLON THE GREAT is fallen…"

Revelation 18:10 "**THAT GREAT CITY BABYLON…**"

Revelation 18:18 "What **CITY** is like unto **THIS GREAT CITY**."

Revelation 18:19 "Alas, alas, **THAT GREAT CITY!**"

Revelation 18:21 "…**THAT GREAT CITY BABYLON…**"\

Revelation 19:2 "…**THE GREAT WHORE**…"

1 Peter 5:13 "The church that is at **BABYLON**, elected together with you, saluteth you… **(Peter was in Jerusalem, Acts 15:2,7)**

The book of Revelation is clearly identifying **ONE GREAT CITY**, which is also referred to as **BABYLON, THE HARLOT, THE WHORE, WHICH IS JERUSALEM!** Revelation draws from the Old Testament more than any other New Testament book. Does the Old Testament speak of **JERUSALEM** in these same terms? (Rev.17:5)

Isaiah 1:21 "How is the **FAITHFUL CITY become** an **HARLOT!**" (An **UNFAITHFUL HARLOT**)

Jeremiah 2:2,20 "…Jerusalem…, playing the **HARLOT**.

Jeremiah 3:1 "…but thou hast played the **HARLOT**…"

Jeremiah 3:3 "thou hadst a **WHORES FOREHEAD**…" ("upon her **FOREHEAD**", Rev.17:5)

Jeremiah 3:6 "…hath played the **HARLOT**."

Jeremiah 3:8 "…went and played the **HARLOT**."

Jeremiah 22:8 "Wherefore hath the Lord done thus unto **THIS GREAT CITY?**

*Nineveh, who came into relationship with God, is once referred to as **that great city.** (Jonah 4:11) They would "rise in judgment with **this generation** (as well), and did condemn it: because they **repented** at the preaching of Jonas; and, behold, a greater than Jonas was there." (Matthew 12:41) Nineveh repented in **40 days** to much lesser of a messenger. **"This generation"** in Jerusalem was given **40 years** to repent, after rejecting a message from the creator of the universe then in killing Him! Oh, the severity of this judgment! "That the blood of all the prophets, which was shed from the foundation of the world, may be required of **this generation!** (Luke 11:50)

This prophecies fulfillment of judgment upon the wicked city of Jerusalem has endless applications today. The harlot (Israel) rode the beast (Rome) and manipulated them (John 19:15) to do the great evils of killing Jesus, the apostles, and millions of Christians!

Revelation 17:5 "And on her forehead a name was written: MYSTERY, BABYLON THE GREAT, THE MOTHER OF HARLOTS AND OF THE ABOMINATIONS OF THE EARTH."

Revelation 17:5

This wicked religious and political antichrist system was a mother.

Mothers give birth to babies! So, there are many copycat murderous religious combined with the Political systems! Again, leftism is a religion, where the government is God! Islam is another example of such, as the murderers believe that they are in the right.

John 16:2 "… ".the time is coming that whoever kills you will think that he offers God service."

And just a side note here. If the inspired word of God is clear about the judgment in the book of Revelation being upon Babylon/The Great City/Jerusalem, and that it was to occur shortly and the time was near (Revelation 1:1,3, 22:10), then the date of the writing of the prophecy occurred prior to AD 70. If you truly believe in the inspiration of scripture, this has to be the case, otherwise it was not a prophecy, but an after the fact meaningless conglomeration of symbolic metaphors concerning a past event.

CHAPTER 18

MATTHEW 24:17,18

FLEEING TO PELLA, NOT ESCAPING IN A RAPTURE.

Matthew 24:17,18 says,

"let him which is on the house top not come down to take anything out of his house: neither let him which is in the field return back to take his clothes."

We don't hang out on the top of our houses today, unless you're a gazillionaire in Newport Beach. This was how homes were made in Jerusalem in the first century, "…Peter went up upon the housetop to pray about the sixth hour:" (Acts 10:9)

Again, these were part of the fleeing instructions given by Jesus. Note that they did flee to Pella in the mountains, according to Eusebius to escape these things.

In Luke 21:36, we read, "Watch ye therefore, and pray always, that ye may be accounted worthy to escape all these things that shall come to pass, and to stand before the Son of man."

This same event occurs in Revelation.

Revelation 12: "Then the woman fled into the wilderness where she had a place prepared by God, so that there she would be nourished for 1,260 days."

That is 3 ½ years.

Note that this has nothing to do with a "beam me up Scotty", Sci-Fi eschatology!

If these events are worldwide, why would Jesus say "then let them which be in Judaea flee to the mountains (Matthew 24:16) and you're good? In an era of F-35's and nuclear weapons, those instructions would be ridiculous!

CHAPTER 19

MATTHEW 24:19,20

FIRST CENTURY PREGNANT WOMEN AND SABBATH TRAVEL LAWS.

Matthew 24:19

"But WOE TO THOSE WHO ARE PREGNANT and to those who are NURSING BABIES in THOSE DAYS!"

To interpret scripture with scripture here reveals the most undeniable fulfillment in the first century!

Luke 23:28-30 says, "But Jesus, turning to them, said, "DAUGHTERS OF JERUSALEM, do not weep for Me, but WEEP FOR YOURSELVES AND FOR YOUR CHILDREN. For indeed THE DAYS are coming in which they will say, 'BLESSED ARE THE BARREN WOMBS THAT NEVER BORE, AND BREASTS WHICH NEVER NURSED!' Then they will begin 'to say to the mountains, "Fall on us!" and to the hills, "Cover us!" ""

The same nursing mothers are being warned here, first century "DAUGHTERS OF JERUSALEM", in the same "DAYS"!

Matthew 24:20 "And pray that your flight may not be in winter or on the Sabbath."

First century travel laws were in effect for Sabbath days in Israel!

Note that the portion of this passage that says, "They will begin to say to the mountains, ""Fall on us", and to the hills, "Cover us" is also in Revelation 6:16, which are quotes taken from Hosea 10:8 and Isaiah 2:19 used in both passages! Therefore, it is connecting the passages to the same event. General Flavius Josephus was found in one such cave (Revelation 6:15)!

CHAPTER 20

MATTHEW 24:21,22

THE GREAT TRIBULATION

Matthew 24:21

"For then there will be great tribulation, such as has not been since the beginning of the world until this time, no, nor ever shall be."

This is from Daniel 12:1 "…And there shall be a time of trouble, Such as never was since there was a nation, Even to that time. And at that time your people shall be delivered, Everyone who is found written in the book."

Concerning THE GREAT TRIBULATION, Jesus told his first century disciples, **"And YOU shall be hated of all men for my name's sake: but he that endureth to the end shall be saved"** (Matthew 10:22)

Jesus then says the same thing to them, verbatim, in **Matthew 24:9,13, "…and YOU (Not "they" in 2K years) shall be hated of all nations for my name's sake…But he that shall endure unto the end, the same shall be saved."**

He then tells us **when** this tribulation would occur in verse 34 of the chapter, **"This generation shall not pass, till ALL THESE THINGS be fulfilled"** (Matthew 24:34).

Verse 21 is prior to verse 34 and is the tribulation, which is part of ALL THESE THINGS. Matthew 24:21 "for then shall be GREAT TRIBULATION, such as was not since the beginning of the world to this time, no, nor ever shall be."

This was the worst tribulation for the old covenant people in that land.

Note, that there is no more Old Covenant in effect, it has passed away (Hebrews 8:13). Since it no longer exists, there are no old covenant people. All such records were burned, by the sovereign hand of God, when the temple was destroyed in AD 70! Thus, you "must be born again" (John 3:3) and have your name written in heaven (Luke 10:20, Revelation 21:27.

Is Jesus a false prophet, not the Messiah, nor God in the flesh, or did He prophesy accurately of the tribulation being in the lifetime of His disciples in the first century?

You are given no other options!

John said that he was in the tribulation, **"I JOHN, your brother and fellow partaker IN THE TRIBULATION" (Revelation 1:9).**

Note that the older manuscripts use the definite Greek article "ho" (the). The KJV manuscripts aren't as old and accurate and leaves it out. Ironically, John Darby says "THE TRIBULATION" in his translation.

Paul tells believers to **not even get married** at that time, because of **"the present distress" (1 Corinthians 7:26)**, the tribulation.

John the Baptist saw this coming upon Israel when he said, "Who has warned you to FLEE the WRATH TO COME" (Matthew 3:7)

Paul saw it when he said, concerning first century persecuting Jews, "WRATH HAS COME UPON THEM TO THE UTTERMOST" (1 Thessalonians 2:16)

Paul says it here as well, "Jesus who delivers us from THE WRATH TO COME" (1 Thessalonians 1:10)

This is not referring to a crapture but FLEEING the WRATH TO COME that John the Baptist mentioned, ""Then let those who are in Judea FLEE to the mountains, let those who are in the midst of her depart, and let not those who are in the country enter her." (Luke 21:21)

116

This was the escape route to avoid the wrath, FLEE the city for the mountains, which Christians did at Pella. (Luke 21:36)

Luke says it again a couple verses later, "...For there will be great distress in the land and WRATH UPON THIS PEOPLE." (Luke 21:23)

Matthew 24:22 "And if those days had not been cut short, no life would have been saved; but for the sake of the elect those days will be cut short."

If the Romans had continued to slaughter, not a single Jew would have remained alive. They did stop and it is estimated that around 100,000 were spared and taken into slavery. No global nuclear conflagration is going on in this verse!

CHAPTER 21

MATTHEW 24:23-26

LOOKING FOR THE INCARNATED CHRIST AND FALSE CHRISTS.

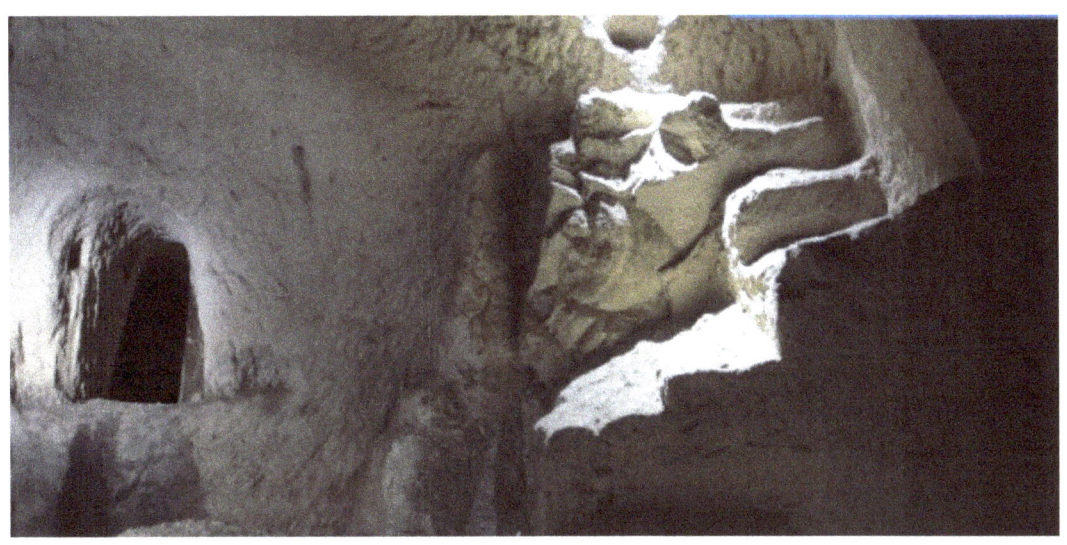

Matthew 24:23

"Then if any man shall say unto you, LO HERE is Christ, or THERE; believe it not."

Jesus reveals to us with these same words concerning the nature of His kingdom in Luke 17 and John 4. John 17:20-22 says, "And when he was demanded of the Pharisees, when the kingdom of God should come, he answered them and said, The kingdom of God cometh not with observation: neither shall they say, LO HERE! or, LO THERE! for, behold, the kingdom of God is within you. And he said unto the disciples, The days will come, when you shall desire to see one of the days of the Son of man, and you shall not see it." They are told that they're not going to be observing Jesus as the king in the kingdom with the natural eye seeing a 5'6, if you will, Jewish rabbi in a robe! Jesus corrects their natural and carnal minds to let them know that they will long to see Him in the flesh as a physical king, "and you shall not see it"!

In John 4:21, we read, "Jesus said to her, "Woman, believe Me, an hour is coming when neither IN THIS MOUNTAIN nor IN JERUSALEM will you worship the Father."

The natural and carnal religious mind wants a location for the kingdom!

118

Mecca, Rome, Salt Lake City, are such examples that we see today. Each city has its own temple, false prophet, and book (s).

Deception comes when one is looking for a physical Jesus in His kingdom in a specific location (Such as the Middle East), as is revealed in the next verses of the Olivet Discourse.

Matthew 24:24 "For there shall arise false Christs, and false prophets, and shall shew great signs and wonders; insomuch that, if it were possible, they shall deceive the very elect."

We see the deceiving going on in verse 5. False Christs and false signs and wonder is addressed clearly by Adam Clark in his commentary. Clark states,

"Josephus in his history: ANT. b. xx. c. 7. Among these Simon Magus, and Dositheus, mentioned before; and Barcocab, who, St. Jerome says, pretended to vomit flames. And it is certain these and some others were so dexterous in imitating miraculous works that they deceived many; and such were their works, that if the elect, the chosen persons, the Christians, had not had the fullest evidence of the truth of Christ's mission and miracles, they must have been deceived too: but, having had these proofs, they could not possibly be deceived by these impostors. This is simply the meaning of this place; and it is truly astonishing that it should be brought as a proof for the doctrine (whether true or false is at present out of the question) of the necessary and eternal perseverance of the saints! How abundant the Jews were in magic, divination, sorcery, incantation, & see proved by Dr. Lightfoot on this place."

Matthew 24:25 *"Behold, I have told YOU (not, "THEM") before".* YOU'VE been warned!

Matthew 24:26 *"So if they say to you, 'Behold, He is in the wilderness,' do not go out; or, 'Behold, He is in the inner rooms,' do not believe them."*

Acts 21:38 *"Then you are not the Egyptian who some time ago stirred up a revolt and led the four thousand men of the Assassins out INTO THE WILDERNESS?"*

Adam Clark reveals the history involved here very well. "If they shall say unto you, Behold, he is in the desert — Is it not worthy of remark that our Lord not only foretold the appearance of these impostors, but also the manner and circumstances of their conduct? Some he mentions as appearing in the desert. Josephus says, ANT. b. xx. c. 7, and WAR, book ii. c. 13: That many impostors and cheats persuaded the people to follow them to the desert, promising to show them signs and wonders done by the providence of God, is well attested. An Egyptian false prophet, mentioned by Josephus, ANT. b. xx. c. 7, and in Acts 21:38, led out into the DESERT four thousand men, who were murderers, but these were all taken or destroyed by Felix. Another promised salvation to the people, if they would follow him to the DESERT, and he was destroyed by Festus, ANT. b. xx. c. 7. Also, one Jonathan, a weaver, persuaded a number to follow him to the DESERT, but he was taken and burnt alive by Vespasian. See WAR, b. vii. c. 11."

CHAPTER 22

MATTHEW 24:27,28

Coming in judgement for all to see them TAKEN as corpses, not in a rapture. Be LEFT alive, not behind!

Roman Legion symbol

Matthew 24:27

"For as the lightning cometh out of the east, and shineth even unto the west; so shall also the COMING of the Son of man be."

As in verse 23, looking for the incarnate individual 5'6 Jesus leads to deception, "believe it not"! His coming would be for all to "see", as in oh, I see, I understand that this is Jesus coming in judgement. All can see lightening over the skies, but they can't see the individual 5'6 Jesus in the sky. Just the logistics and optics here is a ridiculous notion! Lightening is seen by all in a city, and it strikes fast, and is the arrow of His judgment, "his arrow shall go forth as the lightning "(Zechariah 9:14). The Lord's arrow against the evil nation came through the Roman armies, who literally invaded from "the east...to the west"!

Matthew 24:28, "For wheresoever the carcass is, THERE WILL THE EAGLES BE GATHERED TOGETHER", again, let's follow the simple rule of interpreting scripture with scripture. The parallel passage is found in the synoptic gospel of Luke.

Luke 17:34-37 "...one TAKEN, and the other left...one TAKEN, and the other left...Two men shall be in the field; the one shall be TAKEN, and the other left. And they answered and said unto him, WHERE Lord? And he said unto them, Wheresoever the body is, THERE WILL THE EAGLES BE GATHERED TOGETHER." Simple 6th grade English here, where are they taken?

These passages cannot be separated as the words are exactly the same. To do so would be to wrongly divide the word of truth! Quick note, verse 27 comes before verse 34 in Matthew 24, which tells us that, "This generation shall not pass, till all these things be fulfilled".

The connection of Matthew 24:28 and Luke 17:34-37 is further solidified later in the chapter, Matthew 24:39-41 "and knew not until the FLOOD came, and TOOK them all away; so shall also the coming of the Son of man be. Then shall two be in the field; the one shall be TAKEN, and the other left. Two women shall be grinding at the mill; the one shall be TAKEN, and the other left."

We just read Luke 17, where Jesus was bringing to remembrance past judgments and Noah's flood was one of them in Luke 17:26. So, connect all three passages (Ecc.4:12) and those who are taken are taken as carcasses (Matthew 24:27). "The Body" in Luke 17:37 is a dead body, a carcass. And those taken in the flood Matthew 24:39-41, became carcasses. In all three passages, they were TAKEN in judgment, not in a preposterous rapture! The entire Left Behind series is 180 degrees from the truth! This should tell you something about the message behind "Left Behind" the book series! If you have ears to hear, it's opposite of the truth! I may start a book series, "I Want To Be Left Behind, and Spared from Judgment"! The sequel can be, "I Want to be Left Alive"! Even John Walvoord from Dallas Theological cemetery (not a typo) concedes that "one taken and one left" is referring to those being taken in judgment by the Roman Armies. The eagle symbol was used in every aspect of the Roman military. The soldiers were eagles, they had eagles tattooed on their arms, they hoisted various eagle artifacts into battle, on flag poles, eagles everywhere!

From the Movie, "The Eagle" with Channing Tatum, "The eagle is not a piece of metal, the eagle is Rome".

CHAPTER 23

MATTHEW 24:29

THE SUN, MOON AND STARS.

Matthew 24:29

"Immediately after the I tribulation of those days shall the sun be darkened, and the moon shall not give her light, and the stars shall fall from heaven, and the powers of the heavens shall be shaken:"

Some commentators try to say that all the previous verses up to verse 29 are addressing the destruction of Jerusalem in AD 70, but verse 29 then goes into the distant future talking about the end of the world. The first words of this verse debunk such an idea," Immediately after the tribulation of those days". There is no two-thousand-year gap between verses 28 and 29 here!

Verse 29 takes place immediately after verse 28. Note too, that verse 34 says that verse 29 comes prior to Jesus' words of, "This generation shall not pass, till ALL THESE THINGS be fulfilled (Matthew 24:34).

Verse 29 a quote from Isaiah.

Isaiah 13:10, "For the stars of heaven and the constellations thereof shall not give their light: the sun shall be darkened in his going forth, and the moon shall not cause her light to shine."

All commentators would agree that this is a prophecy concerning the judgment of Babylon (Isaiah 13:1), which was carried out through the Medes and Persians (Isaiah 13:17), which was to be the next world governing empire in Daniel's Great Image (Daniel 2:31-45).

So, if this prophecy was fulfilled concerning the judgment of Babylon by the Medes, what of the description of the sun, moon, and stars? All would agree that nothing transpired in the prophecy to the physical sun, moon, and stars. Therefore, why would this change when Jesus, the prophet of prophets, quotes it in Matthew 24:29?

Prophetic and apocalyptic language often uses such imagery to make the point concerning rule. It was first the natural rule of the sun, to rule the day, and the moon and stars to rule the night given to us in Genesis 1:16. After this we see the imagery of these natural forces communicating ruling amongst peoples. In Joseph's dream we see this exact thing.

Genesis 37:9 "And he dreamed yet another dream, and told it his brethren, and said, Behold, I have dreamed a dream more; and behold, the SUN and the MOON and the eleven STARS made obeisance to me." The Sun was his father's authority, the moon, his mother's, and the stars, his brothers. They would all bow to his authority and rule.

Ezekiel 32:7,8 "And when I shall put thee out, I will cover the heaven and make the STARS thereof dark; I will cover the SUN with a cloud and the MOON shall not give her light. All the bright lights of heaven will I make dark over thee, and set darkness upon thy land, saith the Lord God." This passage is describing a judgment against Pharaoh king of Egypt (Ezekiel 32:2). Did anything described here happen in the physical heavens, to the sun, moon, and stars, when Pharaoh was judged? No, it was lights out for Pharaoh's glory and rule

125

AMOS 8:9 "And it shall come to pass in that day, saith the Lord God, that I will cause the SUN to go down at noon, and I will darken the earth (land) in the clear day." This is a judgment against the land of Israel, where her glory and light would be put out and brought down!

So, the sun, moon, and stars are not referring to astronomy in prophetic verbiage. Remember that if a single star struck the earth it would be obliterated. We see the same language in Rev.6:13 with stars striking the earth /land.

Jeremiah 15:9 says, in regard to a judgment upon Jerusalem (vs.5) that, "HER SUN is gone down". Another prophecy concerning the sun, which had nothing to do with the physical sun. Think of the Elton John song, "Don't Let the Sun Go Down on Me".

OBADIAH 4 *"Though thou exalt thyself as the eagle, and though thou set thy nest among the stars, thence will I bring thee down, saith the Lord."*

This prophecy is concerning a judgment upon Edom (vs1).

MICAH 3:6 "Therefore night shall be unto you, that ye shall not have a vision; and it shall be dark unto you, that ye shall not divine; and the SUN shall go down over the prophets, and the day shall be dark over them."

Did physical darkness come over them? All would agree to say, "NO!" This was a call for judgment to be upon Israel's leaders (Micah 3:1)

ECCLESIASTES 12:1,2 "…in the days of thy youth…While the SUN, or the light, or the MOON, or the STARS be not darkened, nor the CLOUDS return after the rain." This usage of the sun, moon, and stars, communicates once again the strength and authority in one's youth. It is not communicating astronomy.

In Acts 2:16-21 we have such mentioning of the sun, moon, and stars, a prophecy that is said to be fulfilled in that day, "this is that which was spoken by the prophet Joel…." Note that it does not say "this is part of that…" Simply, "this, that you're seeing is what that passage in Joel prophesied about"!

Acts 2:16-21 "But this is that which was spoken by the prophet Joel; And it shall come to pass in the last days, saith God, I will pour out of my Spirit upon all flesh: And your sons and your daughters shall prophesy, And your young men shall see visions, And your old men shall dream dreams: And on my servants and on my handmaidens I will pour out in those days of my Spirit;

and they shall prophesy: And I will shew wonders in heaven above, And signs in the earth beneath; Blood, and fire, and vapor of smoke: The SUN shall be turned into darkness, And the MOON into blood, Before that great and notable Day of the Lord come: And it shall come to pass, that whosoever shall call on the name of the Lord shall be saved."

Even today most flags around the world use this imagery of a sun, moon, or stars symbolizing ruling authority of the day, or night. "Falling stars", of course, symbolize a rapid descent, falling from a place of glory, honor, authority and power.

CHAPTER 24

MATTHEW 24:30

GET YOUR HEAD OUT OF THE CLOUDS!

Matthew 24:30

"And then shall appear the sign of the Son of man in heaven: and then shall all the tribes of the earth mourn, and they shall see the Son of man coming in the clouds of heaven with power and great glory."

This verse is a quote from Daniel 7:13, which says, "I kept looking in the night visions, And behold, with the clouds of heaven One like a son of man was coming, And He came up to the Ancient of Days And was presented before Him."

First note that Jesus' coming reveals that His direction is one of going UP to the Ancient of Days". He is not heading down to earth in clouds. Futurism has this backwards, like most everything else in its confusion! This verse is revealing the vindication (Isaiah 61:2, Luke 21:20) and the exaltation of Jesus!

Part of this verse is a quote from Zechariah 12:10, which is also quoted in Revelation 1:7

Young's Literal Translation gets it right here in translating it "TRIBES OF THE LAND", which Adam Clark believes to be accurate as well. And even John Darby says "TRIBES OF THE LAND" in his translation!

Revelation 1:7 reveals that those who are mourning are those who pierced Him! Therefore, there were those tribes in that land that pierced Jesus! The cross was a first century event! Those tribes that carried this about were in that day, not in our day! There are no such tribes in our day. This is the same judgment as Matthew 25:32 (Connect Matthew 25:31, 26:64,19:28, Titus 3:5, and Rev.20:4), which chapter cannot be separated from chapter 24. That would be wrongly dividing the word of truth with chapter breaks that are uninspired themselves.

Revelation 1:7 "Lo, he doth come with the clouds, and see him shall every eye, even those who did pierce him, and wail because of him shall all the TRIBES OF THE LAND Yes! Amen!" YLT

Note again that those twelve tribes of Israel aren't around today and this scripture is saying that these peoples are the very ones that pierced Jesus! These are first-century tribes.

Acts 2:36 "Therefore let all the house of Israel know assuredly that God has made this Jesus, WHOM YOU CRUCIFIED, both Lord and Christ".

And every eye did see Jesus come in clouds of judgement upon Jerusalem in AD 70. Just as the world "saw" the greatest military on earth suffer loss to the United States in the Revolutionary war.

CLOUDS communicate the judgment of God throughout scripture. Caiaphas knew the Old Testament scriptures and reveals that this was a common understanding amongst first century Jews.

Matthew 26:64 "Jesus saith to him and the Sanhedrin, 'Thou hast said; nevertheless I say to you, hereafter YOU shall SEE the Son of Man sitting on the right hand of the power, and **COMING** upon the **CLOUDS** of the heaven.'"

Caiaphas' response was to tear His clothes and make the charge of Blasphemy, because only God Himself would come in the clouds to execute judgment! Jesus was saying here that He was that God of the Old Testament! They were executing judgment upon Him, and Jesus reverses things to say that He was going to execute judgment upon them as God Himself!

This was them "SEEING" Jesus come!

Matthew 16:28 "There be some standing here, which shall not taste of death, till they SEE the Son of man coming in His kingdom".

Titus 2:13 "LOOKING FOR that blessed hope, and the glorious APPEARING of the great God, and our savior Jesus Christ ".

Hebrews 9:28 "…and UNTO THEM THAT LOOK FOR HIM shall He APPEAR a second time without sin unto salvation".

So, if one was not properly looking, one could miss this appearing!

It appeared evident to all, which believed Jesus' words, that it was King Jesus who was sending "His armies (my servants), destroying those murderers and burning up their city" (Matthew 22:7)

Do you SEE what I'm saying here? To do so involves one's ability to understand, perceive, and discern a matter. Nothing to do with physical eyesight. "I once was blind, but now I see" means exactly this in the great hymn Amazing Grace, as do the words of Jesus, ""Jesus said to them, "If you were blind, you would have no sin; but now that you maintain, 'We see,' your sin remains." (John 9:41) and "Leave them alone; they are blind guides of blind people. And if a person who is blind guides another who is blind, both will fall into a pit." (John 15:14) Jesus is NOT referring to the Pharisees physical blindness, but to their spiritual blindness.

COMING IN THE CLOUDS throughout the Old Testament.

Isaiah 19:1"The burden of Egypt. Behold, the LORD rideth upon a swift **CLOUD**, and shall **COME** into Egypt: and the idols of Egypt shall be moved at HIS PRESENCE, and the heart of Egypt shall melt in the midst of it."

Again, COMING in the New Testament (Matthew 24:3) is often the Greek word "**Parousia**", which is defined as "**COMING PRESENCE**"!

All would agree that Isaiah 19:1 was a prophetic judgement upon Egypt and that God was not appearing physically in a cloud to carry out His judgement upon them!

Psalm 104:3 Who layeth the beams of his chambers in the waters: who maketh the **CLOUDS** his chariot: who walketh upon the wings of the wind:"

Are the Holy Spirit inspired scriptures saying that God physically rides in the clouds?

Joel 2:1,2 "Blow ye the trumpet in Zion, and sound an alarm in my holy mountain: let all the inhabitants of the land tremble: for the day of the Lord is **COMING,** for it is nigh at hand; A day of darkness and of gloominess, a day of **CLOUDS** and of thick darkness…" No questions here about **CLOUDS OF JUDGMENT**.

Isaiah 64:1-3 "Oh that thou wouldest rend THE HEAVENS, that thou wouldest **COME** down, that the mountains might flow down at thy **PRESENCE**, As when the melting fire burneth, the fire causeth the waters to boil, to make thy name known to thine adversaries, that the nations may tremble at thy **PRESENCE!** When thou didst terrible things which we looked not for, you **CAME** down, the mountains flowed down at thy **PRESENCE."** No clouds here, but His **COMING PRESENCE (Parousia)** in judgment.

Ezekiel 30:3, 4 "For the day is near, even the day of the Lord is near, a **CLOUDY DAY**; it shall be the time of the heathen. And **THE SWORD SHALL COME** upon Egypt…" Again, **CLOUDS** are used to describe coming judgment, by the sword, upon a nation. That is, by the armies of another nation.

Ezekiel 32:7 "And when I shall put thee out, I will cover the heaven and make the stars thereof dark; I will cover the sun with a **CLOUD**, and the moon shall not give her light," It was lights out for Pharaoh, king of Egypt. (vs.2)

Ezekiel 38:16 "And thou shalt come up against my people of Israel, as a **CLOUD** to cover the land;" An invading army is described as a "**CLOUD**."

Ecclesiastes 12:1,2 "Remember now thy Creator in the days of thy youth, while…the sun, or the light of the moon, or the stars, be not darkened, nor the **CLOUDS** return after the rain:" "The **CLOUDS** returning" is a negative thing here, which as we've seen above, could only be referring to judgment.

Micah 1:3 "For, behold, the Lord is **COMING** forth out of his place, and will **COME** down, and tread upon the high places of the earth." No clouds here but coming down to make things right by abasing the exalted.

So, when the Holy Spirit inspired apostles use this same imagery, as Jesus Himself did here in Matthew 24:30, are they meaning something different than what the whole of scripture is referring to?

Matthew 16:28 "Verily I say unto you, There be some standing here, which shall not taste of death, till they see the Son of man **COMING IN HIS KINGDOM**."

Some of them listening would not die, till they saw Jesus coming in His kingdom! Jesus is not referring to the transfiguration in the next chapter, as that was only 6-8 days later (Matthew 17:1-6)! It makes a mockery of Jesus to say that He prophesied that SOME of you will not die within the next week! This interpretation would mean that some of them would die within the next week. Make any of this make sense! But the fact that most of them would be martyred, yet some would still be alive by the time of Jesus' coming in judgement in AD 70 times out perfectly!

Matthew 10:23 "But whenever they persecute you in one city, flee to the next; for truly I say to you, you will not finish going through the cities of Israel until **THE SON OF MAN COMES**."

Same exact verbiage of The Son of Man COMING. Same coming, same timeline of that coming, in their lifetimes!!!!!

Now consider the prophetic language of the prophet David (Acts 2:30) as he describes God delivering him from Saul. The physical elements being described here would make the natural minded man (1 Corinthians 2:14) think that the severest of weather forecasts was coming at the same time that natural disasters were taking place!

Psalm 18:6-17 "In my distress I called upon the Lord, And cried to my God for help; He heard my voice from His temple, And my cry for help before Him came into His ears. ¶Then the earth shook and quaked; And the foundations of the mountains were trembling And were shaken, because He was angry. Smoke went up out of His nostrils, And fire from His mouth was devouring; Coals burned from it. He also **BOWED THE HEAVENS DOWN LOW** and came down With thick darkness under His feet. He rode on a cherub and flew; And He sped on the wings of the wind. He made darkness His hiding place, His canopy around Him, Darkness of waters, THICK

CLOUDS. From the brightness before Him passed His **THICK CLOUDS**, Hailstones (Revelation 16:21) and coals of fire. The Lord also thundered in the heavens, And the Most High uttered His voice, Hailstones and coals of fire. He sent out His arrows, and scattered them, And lightning flashes in abundance, and routed them. Then the channels of water appeared, And the foundations of the world were exposed By Your rebuke, Lord, At the blast of the breath of Your nostrils. He sent from on high, He took me; He drew me out of many waters. He saved me from my strong enemy, And from those who hated me, for they were too mighty for me."

Another go to verse used to argue for a physical Jesus in the clouds is Acts 1:9-11"And when he had spoken these things, while they beheld, he was taken up; and a cloud received him out of their sight. And while they looked stedfastly toward heaven as he went up, behold, two men stood by them in white apparel; which also said, Ye men of Galilee, why stand ye gazing up into heaven? this same Jesus, which is taken up from you into heaven, shall so come IN LIKE MANNER in as ye have seen him go into heaven."

TROPOS is the Greek word used for "IN LIKE MANNER. This is where we get the word TROPE and TROPOLOGY! The FIGURATIVE use of language!

Tropos is defined as a turn, i.e. (by implication) mode or style (especially with preposition or relative prefix as adverb, like); FIGURATIVELY, deportment or character:—(even) as, conversation, (⊞ like) manner, (⊞ by any) means, way.

Tropos is also used in Matthew 23:37, "...how often would I have gathered thy children together, even AS (Tropos) a hen gathereth her chickens under her wings, and ye would not!" No literal chickens here, but a description of a spiritual reality. There goes Jesus spiritualizing everything! "Gary, you're just spiritualizing the Bible"! Um, yes, "...the words that I speak unto you, they are spirit, and they are life (John 6:63)."

Again, Acts 1:9-11 has Jesus coming in CLOUDS. Why should this mean something different concerning Jesus coming in clouds than what Matthew 24:30 says using the same words? You cannot separate these two passages. Only those who wrongly divide the word of truth do so!

So, if Jesus comes in here in Matthew 24:30, what of communion?

1 Corinthians 11:26 "For as often as you eat this bread and drink this cup, you proclaim the Lord's death TILL He comes."

TILL does not carry in it the meaning of termination of the activity.

1 Corinthians 15:25 "For He must reign TILL He has put all enemies under His feet."

The activity of Jesus reigning does not terminate after His enemies are put under His feet.

If I say, "They walked over the hill TILL I could see them no more". The activity of walking is not terminated with "till" Jesus was with believers till the turbulent end of the Old Covenant age.

Matthew 28:20 "teaching them to observe all, whatever I did command you,) and lo, I am with you all the days —TILL the full end of the age.'"

Does this mean the Jesus would not be with them after the end of the turbulent end of the Old Covenant age? No!

CHAPTER 25

MATTHEW 24:31

TRUMPET GATHERING

Matthew 24:31

"And he shall send his messengers with a great sound of a trumpet, and they shall gather together his chosen from the four winds, from the ends of the heavens unto the ends thereof." YLT

Robert Young translates this correctly here as well. It is MESSENGERS, not angelic beings. God never commissioned angelic beings to preach the gospel and gather peoples into Jesus Christ! Adam Clark says this in his commentary as well. Clark states. "He shall send his angels — τους αγγελους, his messengers, the apostles, and their successors in the Christian ministry."

The Greek word here for "gathering"is episynágō, meaning a place to gather together. It's where we get the word synagogue. As we have read, the gospel went to the four winds, north, east, south and west and turned the world upside down (Acts 17:6, Romans 1:8,10:18,16:25,26, Col.1:5,6,23)!

This was the harvest at the end of the Old Covenant age (Mt.13:39).

Matthew 13:30

*"suffer both to grow together till the harvest, and in the time of the harvest I will say to the reapers, **GATHER** up first the tares, and bind it in, to burn it, and the wheat gather up into my storehouse."*

Matthew 13:39

"and the enemy who sowed them is the devil, and the HARVEST is the end of the age, and the reapers are messengers."

Matthew 13:49

*"so shall it be in the full end of the age, the **MESSENGERS** shall come forth and separate the evil out of the midst of the righteous,"*

There is no way on God's green earth that anyone with an ounce of honesty can separate these verses , Matthew 24:30,31 from 1 Thes. 4:15-17 (harpazo, seizing) and 1 Cor.15:52's **TRUMPET.**

To separate the passages for me would go "against conscience", and it should for you

If you find a way to separate them, then you have a loyalty to creeds and councils, and not to the Word of God alone (Sola Scriptura)!

"Unless I am convinced by Scripture and plain reason - I do not accept the authority of the popes and councils, for they have contradicted each other - my conscience is captive to the Word of God. I cannot and I will not recant anything, for to go against conscience is neither right nor safe."

-Martin Luther (1521)"

THE (not "a") COMING of the Lord, the CLOUDS, the GATHERING TOGETHER and the TRUMPET!"

Different comings in different clouds, a different gathering together, sounded off with a different trumpet? Please!

Matthew 24:30,31

*"and then shall appear the sign of the Son of man in heaven: and then shall all the tribes of the land mourn, and they shall see the Son of man **COMING** in the **CLOUDS** of heaven with power*

*and great glory. And he shall send his messengers with a great sound of a **TRUMP**, and they shall **GATHER TOGETHER** his chosen from the four winds, from the ends of the heavens unto the ends thereof."*

2 Thessalonians 2:1 "And we ask you, brethren, in regard to the **COMING PRESENCE** of our Lord Jesus Christ, and of our **GATHERING TOGETHER** unto him,"

1 Thessalonians 4:16,17 "For the Lord himself shall descend from heaven with a shout, with the voice of the archangel, and with the **TRUMP** of God: and the dead in Christ shall rise first: then we who are living, who are remaining over, together with them shall be seized **TOGETHER** in the **CLOUDS** to meet the Lord in the air, and so always with the Lord we shall be;"

1 Corinthians 15:52 "in a moment, in the twinkling of an eye, in the last **TRUMPET**, for it shall sound, and the dead shall be raised incorruptible, and WE shall be changed:"

For the Heresy Hunters and Rapturists that might be interested in truth concerning 1 Thessalonians 4:17, let's just dive a little deeper as we look at the definitions of some of the words in the passage.

To start with, "up" is nowhere in the word "Harpazo", which simply means "to seize", where some translations mistakenly use "caught up".

If you look at the 13 times Harpazo is used in the New Testament, in at least 12 out of the 13 times, it is never describing physical transportation.

To seize or to grab hold of is how it is used in at least 12 of the 13 usages.

The one time that it may be referring to physical transportation is found in Acts 8:39 "and when they came up out of the water, the Spirit of the Lord seized Philip, and the eunuch saw him no more, for he was going on his way rejoicing;"

Adam Clark questions the idea of physical transportation here in his commentary, "Perhaps this means no more than that the Holy Spirit suggested to the mind of Philip that he should withdraw abruptly from the eunuch, and thus leave him to pursue his journey, reflecting on the important incidents which had taken place."

Nevertheless, the vast majority, 12 of 13 times that Harpazo is used in the New Testament, it is absolutely NOT referring to physical transportation!

Let's look at where 1 Thes.4:17 is taking place. It is in the "air" (aer).

Ephesians 2:2, "...according to the prince of the power of the AIR (aer) the spirit that now worketh in the children of disobedience:"

This is taking place in the invisible realm! As is Revelation 9:2, "And he opened the bottomless pit; and there arose a smoke out of the pit, as the smoke of a great furnace; and the sun and the AIR (aer) were darkened by reason of the smoke of the pit." This is describing the release of demons from the pit, in the spirit realm, nothing to do with a physical pit.

The Greek word for air here is "aer", which is not the air in the sky, that is a different word. That Greek word is "ouranos", meaning the sky, where the birds fly (Mt.13:32). Ouranos is the sky above, which is not the meaning of "aer", which is defined as the realm where one breathes unconsciously.

This event took place within believers as prophesied in 2 Thessalonians 1:10, "when he shall come to be glorified IN HIS SAINTS, and to be admired IN all them that believe..."

This prophecy specifies that "WE" and "US", used multiple times, would experience the event, not "THEY" or "THEM", thousands of years later. These Christians would take part in the exaltation and vindication of Jesus (Dan.7:13), as His persecutors were judged.

They rejoiced in Babylon's/The Great City's/Jerusalem's (Rev.11:8) judgment, because they had been avenged (Rev.18:20)! This all happened IN HIS SAINTS (2 Thes.1:10), "when He comes, in that Day, to be glorified IN HIS SAINTS and to be admired among all those who believe, because our testimony among you was believed."

Think of the children of Israel being delivered from their Egyptian persecutors.

Exodus 19:4 "'You yourselves have seen what I did to the Egyptians, and how I bore you on eagles' wings, and brought you to Myself."

They were not air lifted on a giant 747 sized eagle! They were delivered by God from their Egyptian persecutors as He judged them! So too were New Covenant Israelites (Gal.6:16) delivered from their persecutors from "spiritual Egypt", Jerusalem (Rev..11:8/Lk.13:33)!

Know that Jesus prayed against you being air lifted out of here! "I pray NOT that you take them out of the world..." (John 17:15). You and yours are not going anywhere, deal with it! Stop talking about flying out of here in the sweet by and by, someday in the sky, as the stupid "worship song" says! It's really BAIL WORSHIP, wanting to BAIL out of here! And, by the way, in the book of Revelation, John alone is told to "Come up here, and I will show you what must take place after these things." (Revelation 4:1) HE is seeing a vision (1:11) and is called up to see things from God's higher perspective. How can anyone think that this means the airlift of millions of Christians? Can you say, Eisegesis?

Rapturists will say that the word "church" is not used after chapter 3 in the book, therefore that means that millions of people disappear off the face of the earth? Note that the word "God" is not used in the book of Esther, though He's on every page. After chapter 3 "saints" is used and no place in the entire New Testament does the word communicate anything but believers in Jesus, who are in His "church ". The "elect", the "bride", the "wife", and the "woman" are all used after chapter 3, and they are all communicating the church!

The inseparability of Matthew 24:30,31 and 1 Thessalonians 4:17 is undeniable! Do put this in your creedal pipe and smoke it!

If you're going to defend the inspiration of scripture, you better go back to the drawing board to change your uninspired creeds and church councils!

I believe in the "Second Coming", but dispensationalists and partial biblicists do not. As these camps separate these verses, Matthew 24:30 and 1 Thessalonians 4:17, they are left with 2 or 3 "Second Comings". A secret rapture in 1 Thessalonians 4:17, separate from Matthew 24:30 is what causes the problem as well. Vice versa for a final future coming in 1 Thes.4:17 for others.

Here's the implosion of futurism and partial futurism. For the premillennialist, Jesus comes the second time, third with a secret rapture, before the millennium. It is AFTER the thousand mathematical years (Rev.20) that Jesus comes in His thief coming to bring the New Heavens and New Earth (Rev. 21, 2 Peter 3:10)! This leaves us with FOUR comings of Christ for the Pre-trib rapturists! Is anyone still counting at home?

Again, go back to your creedal drawing boards!

I don't depend on a paycheck, support money, or book sales for my survivability! Is this not the problem here?

Heresy Hunters can also hang themselves on the resurrection here.

What is the nature of the expected body for the Christian?

The Holy Spirit tells us.

1 Corinthians 15:44 "IT IS SOWN A NATURAL BODY, IT IS RAISED A SPIRITUAL BODY"! There He goes again, that Holy Spirit, spiritualizing everything (John 6:63)! Think naturally says the natural man (1 Cor.2:13,14)!

Only a spiritual body can last forever in Heaven, as "flesh and blood cannot inherit the kingdom of God" (1 Corinthians 15:50)

Think about it, Moses and Elijah were not ether when they appeared on the mount in Matthew 17:3.

Yes, a spiritual body awaits believers, as they do not become "naked" without a body, but "clothed" with one at physical death (2 Corinthians 4:3,4). The creeds and councils contradict this in saying that believers go to heaven at physical death and are naked without a body!

What did Jesus mean when He said, "Whoever lives and believes in me SHALL NEVER DIE" (John 11:26).

Jesus is not saying that a believer will never physically die.

The ultimate resurrection is coming out of Adam and into Jesus, being born again with a new nature. Why is there a belief that there is a greater resurrection than this?

2 Timothy 1:10 "Jesus Christ who HAS ABOLISHED DEATH". This does not mean that physical death is no more. "Jesus HAS" is past tense.

My pastor in the 80's was Chuck Smith. He taught, not a few times on this matter contrary to the creeds and councils. And I believe he was right. He pointed out that if a physical body rots in the ground, and is converted to grass, eaten by cows, then becomes part of the cows cellular structure, which cow is then eaten by a man, to become part of his cellular structure, then a shark eats that man, and another man eats that shark, and so on and so on. This concept does not hold up! Chuck believed that believers receive a spiritual body at physical death, not a physical one someday. I believe Chuck Smith was right here! Again, "It is sown/planted a natural body; it is raised a spiritual body" (1 Corinthians 15:44).

Martin Luther had this to say on the matter, "It would take a foolish soul to desire its body when it was already in heaven!" - D. Martin Luthers Werke, ed. Tischreden (Weimar, 1912-1921), p.5534, cited by Althaus, op. cit, p.417.

"Now, if one should say that Abraham's soul lives with God but his body is dead, this distinction is rubbish. I will attack it. One must say, The whole Abraham, the whole man, shall live. The other way you tear off a part of Abraham and say, "It lives." (Table Talk, cited by Althaus, op. cit., p.447.)" -Martin Luther

It must be the natural man that is so obsessed with having a natural body of flesh and blood. One passage of scripture used by those preaching such is found in Job.

Job 19:26 "And though after my skin worms destroy this body, Yet in my flesh shall I see God:" KJV.

About 5 Versions say otherwise.

Consider the irony of ironies in the Darby Translation.

Job 19:26 "And if after my skin this shall be destroyed, yet FROM OUT OF MY FLESH shall I see God" -Darby

My Cambridge KJV makes this note, "After I awake, though this body be destroyed, yet OUT OF MY FLESH".

Job 19:26 "When after my skin this is destroyed, then WITHOUT MY FLESH I SHALL SEE GOD". -Masoretic Text (1917).

Without the true meaning of the verse, we are left with a contradiction against the New Testament scriptures.

1 Corinthians 15:50 "Now this I say, brethren, that flesh and blood cannot inherit the kingdom of God; neither doth corruption inherit incorruption."

"Few scholars today see job as a reference to bodily life after death"

N.T. Write

141

Another passage used to try and make the case for physical bodies being resurrected is in Matthew.

Matthew 27:51-53

"And, behold, the veil of the temple was rent in twain from the top to the bottom; and the earth did quake, and the rocks rent; and the graves were opened; and many bodies of the saints which slept arose, and came out of the graves after his resurrection, and went into the holy city, and appeared unto many."

Martin Luther, Epiphanius, Ambrose Calivius, and Origen all argue that these saints are in glorified spiritual bodies.

Note, that for most of church history, teaching against a future physical body being raised was punishable by death. Such "heretics" would be burned to death and all of their scholarly works would be burned with them.

It should tell you something of how strange this doctrine is in that, according to resurrection teachings of the creeds and councils, the process of raising a physical and biological body and then transforming it into a spiritual body would take about one literal second, where the physical body is reassembled and transformed into a spiritual bodyBut if you don't believe in that one literal second, then you are a heretic that has left the faith!

1 Cor.15:4 "and that He was buried, and that He rose again the third day according to the Scriptures,"

Jesus did not see corruption in those prophesied 3 days, as David did (Acts 2:27, 13:35-37, Revelation 13:8). It was plan A to the T, for Jesus to go to the cross and raise exactly 3 days later!

And yes, Jesus was raised from the dead in a physical body after 3 days, as he physically ate and drank after His resurrection. This is the uniqueness of Jesus being the "only begotten Son" (John 3:16). The sole purpose of Jesus' incarnation was to become a sacrifice, "a body you have prepared me" (Hebrews 10:5). God, the eternal Son became a man of flesh and blood for this sole purpose. Again, after His resurrection, He was of flesh and bone" (Luke 24:39). But after His ascension we are told that "flesh and blood cannot inherit the kingdom of God" (1 Corinthians 15:50). Therefore, God the eternal Son had to transition at this point. Remember that after the ascension Jesus appeared to Paul as " a light from heaven" (Acts 9:3), and to John as follows "His head and His hair were white like white wool, like snow; and His eyes were like a flame of fire. His feet were like burnished bronze, when it has been made to glow in a furnace…." (Revelation 1:14-15)

Hebrews 5:7 reveals that Jesus is no longer related to as an approximately 5'6 (average height in the first century) Jewish Rabbi in a robe, "who in the days of His flesh", clearly inferring that He is no longer in His flesh. Martha was told by Jesus not to cling to Him (John 20:17). This is the same correction that Jesus told His disciples when He was going to leave them, but then He would come to them and dwell within them in John 14:3, 18-20. Believer's minds were to be spiritually renewed from thinking naturally. They wanted to see with their natural eye a king in a kingdom that came by observation, but Jesus corrects this thinking as he saw that their natural man longed for it. (Luke 17:20-22).

"The days will come when you will long to see one of the days of the Son of Man, and YOU WILL NOT SEE IT"!

1 Corinthians 2:14 "The natural person does not accept the things of the Spirit of God, for they are folly to him, and he is not able to understand them because they are spiritually discerned."

The natural mind might read the following and think it's referring to physical bodies popping out of their graves.

Ezekiel 37:13

"Then you shall know that I am the Lord, when I have opened your graves, O My people, and brought you up from your graves."

However, this is a prophecy concerning Israel's deliverance from the Babylonian captivity, when they'd be brought back into their own land. Outside that land was considered "death".

This was the same concerning outside the garden in Genesis.

Genesis 2:17 says, "IN THE DAY that you eat thereof, surely you shall die". Adam didn't die physically that day, but thus death was alienation and separation from the life of God". He was also ousted from the land, as we see with Israel in the above verse. This alienation and separation from God is the death that Jesus delivered us from. Jesus becomes that promised land and restores us in covenant relationship with God. Physical healing is only a sign that points to spiritual healing and life. The visible revealing the greater invisible healing and life from the dead.

The Pronoun "WE" in 1 Cor. 15:51 & 1 The. 4:15 by Alpheus Crosby (1850).

"Some suppose that the word 'we' is here used very loosely and that the apostle merely meant to say that there would be some Christians alive, and so changed without death, at the time of Christ's Second Coming. But to this view, there are strong, if not insurmountable, objections.

1. It's at variance with the natural interpretation of the passages. If a pastor, in addressing his people either from the pulpit or by letter, should use such expressions as 'We shall not all die,' 'We who are alive and remain unto the coming of the Lord,' etc., would he not be understood as believing in the speedy coming of Christ? And had the Corinthians or Thessalonians any reason for understanding the apostle differently?

2. It greatly diminishes the force and significance of these passages.

3. It doesn't consist with the emphasis belonging to 'we' in those clauses in which it has been printed [in the Greek] in small capitals. In these clauses, the pronoun is expressed in the original, so that, according to a familiar law of the Greek language, it must be emphatic and used in marked contradistinction. The form of expression in 1 The. 4:15 & 17 is peculiarly strong: we who are living, who are surviving. And...

4. The loose view makes the apostle's consolation to the Thessalonians little more than mere mockery. They were sorrowing for their departed friends. He attempted, therefore, to comfort them by saying, 'We who are living, who are surviving till the coming of the Lord, shall not precede or have any advantage in point of time over those who are asleep.' What an extraordinary mode of consolation to the least if the apostle, and those whom he was addressing, supposed that they might all lie in their graves beside their friends thousands of years before the coming of the Christ! But if they were looking for the speedy appearance, triumph, [etc.] of their Savior while some were fearing that their friends who had died too soon would not be present to take part in the glories and joys of these events, then how natural, appropriate, and forcible does every word of the apostle become!" (The Second Advent, pp. 55-56).

Notice that the multiple uses "we" and "us" in the 1 Thessalonians 4 and 1 Corinthians 15 resurrection prophecy! It's not "they" or "them".

1 Corinthians 15:51,52 "Behold, I shew you a mystery; WE shall not all sleep (Matthew 16:28), but WE shall all be changed, in a moment, in the twinkling of an eye, at the last TRUMP: for the

TRUMPET (1 Thes.4:16) shall sound, and the dead shall be raised incorruptible, and WE shall be changed."

AGAIN, this prophecy cannot be separated from 1 Thessalonians 4:17, which cannot be separated from Matthew 24:30, which took place in Jesus' generation (Matthew 24:34)!

Also, remember that the chapter is talking about the natural man Adam verses the spiritual man Jesus (1 Corinthians 15:22, 45-49). The chapter ends with, "The sting of death is sin, and the power of sin is the Law; but thanks be to God, who gives us the victory through our Lord Jesus Christ." (1 Corinthians 15:56,57). Paul is not pulling this thought out from nowhere. The old man verses the new man is the true meaning of the entire chapter.

Just another quick wrench here. If 1 Thes.4 is a resurrection judgement in our future, how is it that believers are judged at physical death (Hebrews 9:27), but are then to go back in their physical bodies and be judged again in the future? There was a judgment that was "about to (Gk. Mello) judge the living and the dead" (1 Peter 4:5). Once to die and then the judgment, and then another judgment in the distant future?

1 Thessalonians 4:15-17 "For this we say unto you by the word of the Lord, that WE which are alive (Matthew 16:28) and remain unto the coming of the Lord shall not prevent them which are asleep. For the Lord himself shall descend from heaven with a shout, with the voice of the archangel, and with the trump of God: and the dead in Christ shall rise first: then WE which are alive and remain shall be seized together with them in the clouds, to meet the Lord in the air: and so shall WE ever be with the Lord."

I've broken down the chapter above to reveal the definition and usage of seize/caught/ grabbed hold of, "Harpazo" previously in this chapter. When Jesus says concerning His sheep that "neither shall anyone PLUCK (Harpazo) them out of my hand" (John 10:28), it has nothing to do with physical transportation, but something spiritual concerning the heart connected to hearing His voice!

Back to Adam's "death".

Genesis 3:22 "And the LORD God said, Behold, the man is become as one of us, to know good and evil: and now, lest he put forth his hand, and take also of the tree of life, and eat, and live forever:"

This clearly states that Adam had not partaken of the tree of life, so as to live forever. Things had to play out, as Plan A was to bring man out of his natural nature (1 Cor.15:22), Adam, and into the Spiritual Man, Jesus! Plan A, "The Lamb slain from the foundation of the world" (Rev.13:8).

Adam was not going to live forever. The natural man sins and hadn't come out of his faulty nature and into Jesus, the tree of life, so as to live forever! (Genesis 2:9, 3:24, Revelation 2:7, 22:2,14).

Isaiah 26:19 "Your dead will live; Their corpses will rise. You who lie in the dust, awake and shout for joy, For your dew is as the dew of the dawn, And the earth will give birth to the departed spirits."

Now the Holy Spirit goes and spiritualizes the Bible, ("heretic") here to say that this is not referring to a physical resurrection, as He quotes it in Ephesians 5:14, "For this reason it says, "Awake, sleeper, And arise from the dead, And Christ will shine on you."

And Daniel speaks of the resurrection in Daniel 12.

Daniel 12:2,3 *"And many of them that sleep in the dust of the earth shall awake, some to everlasting life, and some to shame and everlasting contempt. (John 5:24-29, "now is"). And they that be wise shall shine as the brightness of the firmament; and they that turn many to righteousness as the stars for ever and ever."*

They're resurrected out of the dust at the end (Time of the end, not end of time), yet they're evangelizing, "and they shall turn many to righteousness"! Again, go back to your credal drawing boards. Or better yet, how about just sticking with Sola Scriptura, only scripture!

Note the timing of Daniel's resurrection.

Daniel 12:1,2 *"At that time Michael shall stand up, The great prince who stands watch over the sons of your people; And there shall be A TIME OF TROUBLE, SUCH AS NEVER WAS SINCE THERE WAS A NATION, Even to that time. And at that time your people shall be delivered, Every one who is found written in the book. And many of those who sleep in the dust of the earth shall awake, Some to everlasting life, Some to shame and everlasting contempt."*

This tribulation is quoted by Jesus in Matthew 24:21, which means it had to have occurred in the first century, as verse 34 is after verse 21, "This generation shall not pass, till all these things be fulfilled" (Matthew 24:34)!

And the timing that entirely refutes futurism is in 21:8 and 1 Peter 4:7.

Luke 21:8 *"And He said: "Take heed that you not be deceived. For many will come in My name, saying, 'I am He,' and, "THE TIME HAS DRAWN NEAR." Therefore, do not go after them."*

Jesus is saying that the happenings of the Olivet Discourse, which includes Daniel's tribulation and resurrection, could be taught prematurely.

We see this happening in 2 Timothy 2:17,18 "And their message will spread like cancer. Hymenaeus and Philetus are of this sort, who have strayed concerning the truth, saying that the resurrection is already past; and they overthrow the faith of some."

First note that if the understanding was individual bodies physically coming up out of graves, there would be no discussion on the matter. "Just look around, off course that didn't happen", would have been the point that quickly refuted such an idea, but that point wasn't made. Hymenaeus and Philetus were off by less than a decade. Today's teaching is off by a couple millennia!

So, Luke says that the timing of these things could be misconstrued by people that would mislead others prematurely, saying that the time is NEAR. BUT Peter then says, nearly 40 years later, something that is not premature, that the time of the end is, indeed, NEAR!

1 Peter 4:7 *"THE END OF ALL THINGS IS NEAR..."*

These two verses absolutely eradicate futurism. Do take your time and meditate on the timing given to us in Luke 21:8 and 1 Peter 4: 7. There is a similar countdown that we see with "the last days" (Acts 2:17, Hebrews 1:2), the last day (John 6:40), and the last hour (1 John 2:18). Note that this is not communicating 24 hours or 60 minutes here.

In one sense, The Resurrection is never past as it is a person, Jesus.

John 11:25 *"I am the resurrection"*

People are being raised from death to life daily, and people are physically dying, and given spiritual bodies every day (1 Cor.15:44).

This same resurrection evangelizing problem that we see in Daniel 12:1-3 exists with evangelizing happening after the New Heavens and New Earth in Revelation 22:17, ""And the

147

Spirit and the bride say, Come. And let him that heareth say, Come. And let him that is athirst come. And whosoever will, let him take the water of life freely."

If the Holy Spirit is calling people to come and receive life, that's not a utopia in Revelation 21 and 22 with the New Heavens and New Earth!

Let's be renewed in our minds what the word of God is communicating with the terms HEAVEN and EARTH!

All of the following usages of these terms is not referring to the physical heavens and earth.

Remember that Daniel said that "The HEAVENS do rule" (Daniel 4:26). He is not saying that the physical elements rule!

Deuteronomy 32:1 *"Give ear, O ye HEAVENS, and I will speak; and hear O EARTH, the words of my mouth". The verse prior reveals to whom Moses is addressing, "And Moses spake in the ears of all THE CONGREGATION OF ISRAEL…" God in HEAVEN is joined with man on EARTH in covenant.*

Isaiah 1:2 *"Hear, O HEAVENS, and give ear, O EARTH, for the Lord has spoken…" Isaiah is addressing Judah and Jerusalem, the covenant people (Isaiah 1:1).*

Isaiah 51:16 *"…that I may plant THE HEAVENS, and lay the foundations of THE EARTH, and say unto ZION, THOU ART MY (COVENANT) PEOPLE." The puritan theologian John Owen uses this verse to explain 2 Peter 3's, "THE HEAVENS AND THE EARTH.*

Psalms 50:4, 5 *"He shall call to THE HEAVENS from above, and to THE EARTH, that He may judge HIS PEOPLE. Gather MY SAINTS together unto me; those that have made a COVENANT with me by sacrifice."*

Hosea 2:18-21 *"And in that day will I make A COVENANT for them…And I will BETROTH (covenant) thee unto me forever…I will even BETROTH (covenant) thee unto me in faithfulness: and thou shalt know the Lord. And it shall come to pass in that day, I will hear, saith the Lord, I will hear THE HEAVENS, and they shall hear THE EARTH."*

Joel 2:30 *"And I will shew wonders in THE HEAVENS and in THE EARTH, blood, and fire, and pillars of smoke." This verse is right in the middle of the passage quoted by Peter in Acts 2:16-21, where Peter says, this (the outpouring of the Spirit at the beginning of the new covenant) is* *that (Joel 2:28-32) which was spoken by the prophet Joel...*" This event is that passage of *scripture's fulfillment! The old heavens and earth of the old covenant system (the temple, city, and nation) would go up in smoke (blood and fire and pillars of smoke - Matthew 22:7) as the new covenant was being established on the earth.*

Joel 3:16 *"The Lord also shall roar out of ZION and utter his voice from JERUSALEM; and THE HEAVENS and THE EARTH shall shake: but the Lord will be the hope of HIS PEOPLE, and the strength of THE CHILDREN OF ISRAEL."*

Isaiah 49:13 *"Sing, O HEAVENS; and be joyful, O EARTH; and break forth into singing, O mountains: for the LORD hath comforted HIS PEOPLE, and will have mercy upon his afflicted." ..."*

Zechariah 12:1 *"The burden of the word of the Lord for ISRAEL, saith the Lord, which stretcheth forth THE HEAVENS and layeth the foundations of THE EARTH, and formeth the spirit of man within him."*

Matthew 5:17,18 is the clearest of all revelation on this matter of "HEAVEN AND EARTH.", given to us by the teacher of teachers.

"Think not that I am come to destroy the law, or the prophets: I am not come to destroy but to fulfill. For verily I say unto you, Till HEAVEN AND EARTH PASS, one jot or one tittle shall in no wise pass from the law, till all be fulfilled. (By Him)

Timing has everything to do with Bible Prophecy Fulfilled. Till is a timing word here. Plain as day here, Once I fulfill the law, the "HEAVEN AND EARTH", of the old covenant, WILL PASS!" The Old Covenant rule upon the earth will pass after He fulfills every jot and and tittle of the law and the prophets. Did he or did Jesus not fulfill every jot and title of the law and the prophets? Yes, He did, therefore HEAVEN ND EARTH HAVE PASSED! His words would not pass (Mt.24:35) but would be the foundation of the New Covenant temple made without hands, a house that would endure all storms (Mt.7:24-27), in an EVERLASTING COVENANT!

Revelation 21:1-5 says that this new temple/tabernacle of God is with men. It is the NEW HEAVEN and NEW EARTH, while the former/old things are PASSED AWAY! Behold, I make ALL THINGS NEW... IT IS DONE! "...A New Covenant He hath made the first OLD. Now that which decayeth and waxeth OLD is ready to (it did pass away in A.D. 70) VANISH AWAY."

(Heb.8:13) The Old tabernacle/temple was about to pass away and the New Temple of Jesus' Body/Temple/Tabernacle/Church was about to be made manifest to all. (Heb.9:8)

2 Cor. 3:7 *"written…in stones…which glory was PASSING AWAY."*

2 Cor. 3:11 *"For if what is PASSING AWAY was glorious…"*

But what about 2 Peter 3? At one point in my investigation, seeking the truth of the Lord in scripture, I was convinced that Matthew 24 was fulfilled, but there was no denying that 2 Peter 3 spoke of Thermo Nuclear war. What I found in the passage changed my life!

As we've just examined "HEAVEN and EARTH, we should now have a completely different understanding from our western minds to that of the Old testament scriptures, as well as the New Testament scriptures which draw from the Old, and their usages of the terms "HEAVEN AND EARTH."

2 Peter 3:10 tells us that *the "…THE HEAVENS SHALL PASS AWAY with a great noise, and the elements shall melt with fervent heat, THE EARTH also and the works that are therein shall be burned up."* Now do these terms mean something different to us after examining the Old Testament's uses of them? This approach to scripture is simply interpreting scripture with scripture. We must stand back and not run with our own thoughts and understandings. We should pause and ask ourselves, "what do we know about this or that term, from the rest of scripture?

But this passage speaks of the "elements" melting and burning up. "Yes, this is talking about thermonuclear war." Wait! Pause! Where else is this term "ELEMENTS" used in the scriptures? Answer, the Greek word is "Stoicheion." Its definition is: Rudiments, philosophies, and principles. It's used only in the following verses in the New Testament.

Galatians 4:3, *"Even so we, when we were children, were in bondage under the ELEMENTS of the world:"*

Galatians 4:9, *"But now that you have come to know God, or rather to be known by God, how is it that you turn back again to the weak and worthless ELEMENTARY PRINCIPLES, to which you want to be enslaved all over again?"* Think of elementary school.

Colossians 2:8 says, *"See to it that there is no one who takes you captive through philosophy and empty deception in accordance with human tradition, in accordance with the ELEMENTARY PRINCIPLES of the world, (Old Covenant arrangement) rather than in accordance with Christ."*

Colossians 2:20 states, *"If you have died with Christ to the ELEMENTARY PRINCIPLES of the world, why, as if you were living in the world, do you submit yourself to decrees, such as,"*

*Note that the "world" here is truly the Old Covenant world and its arrangement. Also, in the Old Covenant arrangement gentiles ruled the world, as seen in Daniel's statue/Great Image. We who are in Christ are truly "Jews" in the Jewish Messiah's Kingdom world (Dan.2, Romans 2:28,29, 9:8, Rev.2:9, 3:9).

Hebrews 5:12 says, *"For though by this time you ought to be teachers, you have need again for someone to teach you the ELEMENTARY PRINCIPLES of the actual words of God, and you have come to need milk and not solid food."*

John Lightfoot (1602-1675) states, concerning 2 Peter 3:10, the following, " The heavens shall pass away with a great noise, and the elements shall melt with fervent heat, &c. Compare this with Deuteronomy 32:22, Hebrews 12:26: and observe that by the elements are understood the Mosaic elements, Galatians 4:9, Colossians 2:20: and you will not doubt that St. Peter speaks only of the conflagration of Jerusalem, the destruction of the Nation, and the abolishing of the dispensation of Moses." (Vol.3 p.452)

The definition and New Testament usage of ELEMENTS (Stoichion) does not allow for the meaning of the physical elements! How freeing the truth is (John 8:32) in delivering us from the lies, thus bondage, that futurism has taught us!

Note that the "last days mockers" in 2 Peter 3:3,4 are Jewish mockers, believers that the Old Covenant creation of their "fathers" would continue and not pass away.

2 Peter 3:3,4 *"Know this first of all, that in the last days mockers will come with their mocking, following after their own lusts, and saying, "Where is the promise of His coming? For ever SINCE THE FATHERS fell asleep, all things continue just as they were from the beginning of creation"*

And those of us seing the fulfillment of this prophecy are not saying "WHERE is the promise of His coming? "We are saying, "THERE is the promise of His coming," exactly when Jesus said it would be, in His generation (Matthew 24:3,34, 10:23, 16:28, Rev. 1:1,3,7,22:10).

C.H. Spurgeon states, "Did you ever regret the absence of the burnt offering, or the red heifer, or any one of the sacrifices and rites of the Jews? No, because though these were like the OLD HEAVENS AND EARTH to the Jewish believers, THEY HAVE PASSED AWAY, AND WE NOW

LIVE UNDER A NEW HEAVENS AND A NEW EARTH, so far as the dispensation of divine teaching is concerned. The substance is come, and the shadow has gone: and we do not remember it." (C.H. Spurgeon, MP vol.38 p. 354)

Note that the earth itself has no end, according to scripture.

Ecclesiastes 1:4 says that "the earth endures forever."

Psalms 78:69..." *like the earth which he hath established forever.*"

Psalms 104:5..." *Who laid the foundations of the earth, that it should not be removed forever.*

Ephesians 3:21..." *Unto him be glory in the church by Christ Jesus through out all ages, world without end. Amen.* (The "Church age" has no end, neither does the planet with which it's upon.)

The Puritan Theologian, John Owen (1616–1683) says the following concerning Heaven and Earth:

"*It is evident, then, that in the prophetical idiom and manner of speech, by heavens and earth, the civil and religious state and combination of men in the world, and the men of them, were often understood. So were the heavens and earth that world which then was destroyed by the flood.*"

Numerous non natural minded scholars of the past have had depth in seeing such things. Today's teachers are the shallowest sensationalist propagators of imagination, which is absolutely absent of pure revelation! There is a hoard of crystal ball like guess work occurring by smooth talking soothsayers and psychic powers seeking to give glory to man!

John Brown (1856) on "Heavens and Earth":

"A person at all familiar with the phraseology of the Old Testament Scriptures knows that the dissolution of the Mosaic economy and the establishment of the Christian is often spoken of as the removing of the old earth and heavens and the creation of a new earth and new heavens (see Isa. 65:17, 66:22, & 2 Pet. 3:13). The period of the close of the one dispensation and the commencement of the other is spoken of as 'the last days' and 'the end of the world,' and is often described as such a shaking of the earth and heavens as should lead to the removal of the things which were shaken (Hag. 2:6 & Heb. 12:26-28)." ("Discourses and Sayings of Our Lord"; Vol. 1, P. 157)

The NEW HEAVENS AND NEW EARTH reveal Jesus and Jesus alone! He's all that, which is not enough for the natural man!

Revelation 22:1,2 *"And he showed me a pure RIVER of water of LIFE, CLEAR as crystal, proceeding from the throne of God and of the Lamb. In the middle of its STREET (Not streets), and on either side of the river, was the tree of life, which bore twelve fruits, each tree yielding its fruit every month. The leaves of the tree were for the healing of the nations."*

It's a RIVER, but it's a STREET, and it's GOLD (21:21), but it is CRYSAL CLEAR and TRANSPARENT GLASS. The natural mind has a tough time with this book!

Jesus is the WAY (STREET), the TRUTH (CLEAR AS CRYSTAL), and the LIFE (WATER OF LIFE). -John 14:6

Oh, you're just saying that this book's prophecy is about Jesus! Yes, "For the testimony of Jesus is the spirit of prophecy" (Revelation 19:10).

Revelation 21:21 *"And the street of the city was pure GOLD, like TRANSPARENT GLASS."*

Again, the naturally minded literalist doesn't see that this is speaking of spiritual things.

1 Corinthians 2:13,14 "When we tell you these things, we do not use words that come from human wisdom. Instead, we speak words given to us by the Spirit, using the Spirit's words to explain spiritual truths. But people who aren't spiritual can't receive these truths from God's Spirit. It all sounds foolish to them and they can't understand it, for only those who are spiritual can understand what the Spirit means."

I'll never forget when I heard dispensationalist David Hocking say that there was going to be a "real" river in Revelation 22. It's not that spiritual river that Jesus spoke of.

John 7:48 *"The one who believes in Me, as the Scripture said, 'From his innermost being will flow RIVERS OF LIVING WATER"*

John 4:10 *"Jesus answered and said to her, "If you knew the gift of God, and who it is who says to you, 'Give Me a drink,' you would have asked Him, and He would have given you LIVING WATER."*

John 4:14 *"but whoever drinks of the water that I will give him shall never be thirsty; but the water that I will give him will become in him a FOUNTAIN OF WATER springing up to eternal life."*

Revelation 21:1,2 *"And he showed me a RIVER OF WATER OF LIFE, clear as crystal, coming from the throne of God and of the Lamb, in the middle of ITS STREET. On either side of the river was the tree of life, bearing twelve kinds of fruit, yielding its fruit every month; and the leaves of the tree were for the healing of the nations."*

There goes Jesus and the Holy Spirit, always spiritualizing everything! David Hocking knows better though.

John 6:63 *"It is the Spirit who gives life; the flesh profits nothing. THE WORDS THAT I SPEAK TO YOU ARE SPIRIT, AND THEY ARE LIFE"*

The physical realm is more real to the natural man, where the spiritual realm is more real to the spiritual man.

So, I wonder if Jesus meant something spiritual when He gave the dimensions of the New Covenant Kingdom's capital city, The New Jerusalem Matthew 5:14 "'Ye are the light of the world, A CITY set upon a MOUNT is not able to be hid;" (YLT)

And what Mount may the Holy Spirit inspired New Testament scriptures might this be referring to?

Hebrews 12:22 *"But, ye came to MOUNT ZION, and to the CITY of the living God, to the heavenly Jerusalem, and to myriads of messengers,"* (YLT)

Is the simplicity of interpreting scripture with scripture here not revealing clear revelation of the heart, mind and plan of God?

So, I wonder if the measurements of the City of God might be along these lines?

Revelation 21:16 *"The city is laid out as a square, and its LENGTH is as great as the WIDTH; and he measured the city with the rod, TWELVE thousand stadia; its length, and HEIGHT are equal."*

Twelve has a prophetic meaning here, twelve apostles (21:14). Many translators miss this and give us 1500 miles of the natural mind.

Ephesians 3:18 *"may be able to comprehend with all the saints what is the WIDTH and LENGTH and HEIGHT and depth,"* There goes that Holy Spirit again, comparing spiritual things with spiritual, causing the natural mind to reject such things (1 Corinthians 2:13,14)!

Think of the simplicity of seeing the New Heavens and New Earth of Revelation 21 and 22 as the New Creation.

The individual New Creation in, 2 Corinthians 5:17 "Therefore if anyone is in Christ, this person is a NEW CREATION; the old things PASSED AWAY; behold, NEW THINGS have come."

The corporate New Creation, Revelation 21:1"Then I saw a NEW heaven and a NEW earth; for the first heaven and the first earth PASSED AWAY and there is no longer any sea."

Think about it, if you observe pictures of outer space, you see beauty. Why do we need new physical heavens? Did it ever sin?

And the Earth, thumb through a National Geographic magazine and you see a beautiful planet! The planet never sinned!

It is the heart of man that has sinned and needs to be removed and replaced with a new one! It's not about the outward environment that needs attention. While on the subject, Jesus did not die for tadpoles!

While discussing the book of Revelation here, a couple key points to realize. There is no physical paradise after the New Heavens and New Earth. There is no need for healing in heaven, "the leaves of the tree were for the healing of the nations" (Revelation 22:2). Neither is there evangelizing in heaven, "The Spirit and the bride say, "Come." And let the one who hears say, "Come." And let the one who is thirsty come; let the one who desires, take the water of life without cost." (Revelation 22:17). Also, neither are there "sorcerers, fornicators, murderers" (Revelation 22:15) around in heaven. Such people physically die, as is also revealed in Isaiah 65:17-20.

Isaiah 65:17 "For behold, I create new heavens and a new earth; And the former things will not be remembered or come to mind". This is quoted in Revelation 21:1

In the New Heavens and New Earth, "the youth will DIE at the age of a hundred" (Isaiah 65:20). Therefore, the New Heavens and Earth are not talking about a utopia in heaven.

So, Revelation 21:4 can't be saying that there is no more physical death on the planet.

155

Revelation 21:4 "and God shall wipe away every tear from their eyes, and the death shall not be any more, nor sorrow, nor crying, nor shall there be any more pain, because the first things did go away.'" (YLT)

This exact verse is quoted in that passage concerning the New Heavens and Earth in Isaiah 65.

Isaiah 65:19 "And I have rejoiced in Jerusalem, And have joyed in My people, And not heard in her any more Is the voice of weeping, and the voice of crying."

This was a common saying in prophetic passages throughout scripture describing deliverance from persecution and captivity.

Isaiah 35:10 "And the redeemed of the Lord will return And come to Zion with joyful shouting, And everlasting joy will be on their heads. They will obtain gladness and joy, And sorrow and sighing will flee away."

Israel would be delivered from Babylon here.

So, the New Covenant Israelites would be delivered from their Babylonian persecutors, BABYLON THE GREAT (Rev.11:8), the Jerusalem harlot who was riding the beast (Rome, Rev.17:3) to carry out the persecution.

It was being persecuted unto the death (John 16:2), by those under the influence of the "ministry of death" (2 Corinthians 3:7), which was the "death" that was to be "no more" in Revelation 21:4.

I remember seeing movies of soldiers in war sleeping in the jungles of Vietnam saying how that they longed for the day when the war was over, no more death, no more miserable living conditions, etc. They were not saying that their hope was for a utopia on the planet where no one ever physically died again.

Revelation 21:4, says *"no more sorrow, nor crying"*. Think of this in the light of,

Psalm 30:5 *"WEEPING may endure for a NIGHT, But joy comes in the morning."*

The first century's persecuted Christians were encouraged through the tribulation with such words as,

Romans 13:12 *"The NIGHT is far spent, the DAY is at hand."*

PS This verse has timing in it! As does the following verse.

2 Peter 1:19 *"And so we have the prophetic word confirmed, which you do well to heed as a light that shines in a dark place, UNTIL THE DAY DAWNS AND THE MORNING STAR RISES IN YOUR HEARTS".*

While addressing Some of the misunderstandings in Revelation, know that Satan was judged, condemned, dethroned, and defeated, but not annihilated.

Revelation 20:10 *"And the devil who deceived them was thrown into the lake of fire and brimstone, where the beast and the false prophet are also; and they will be tormented day and night forever and ever."*

The fire here speaks of the judgment of God. Satan has been judged and is "a defeated foe" as Martin Luther put it, yet he's not annihilated. God has always allowed for there to be darkness and light (Genesis 1:4) before the physical creation of light. It's still there in the last chapter of the Bible as well, as outside the city are fornicators and murderers (Rev. 22:15). This, somehow, has to do with God's love, which is received or rejected. Otherwise, forced "love" is not love, but something robotic in nature.

So, yes, I do believe that Satan was judged in "the lake of fire", because God said that this prophecy was going to be fulfilled "soon" and it was "At hand/near" (Revelation 1:1,3,22:10) in the first century. This is what's called believing the word of God. I believe in the inspiration, inerrancy, and infallibility of the word of God. Futurists do not. I encourage futurists to change the way they think/repent and believe His word. Believe the revelation of His word and turn from the imaginations of man in futurism!

I do not wear the label of a "Full Preterist", as that is often accompanied with cessationism, which I address in the Addendum at the end of the book. I believe that many preterists offer an engine with the most powerful and intricate details to design the most efficient ride possible, only to not include the spark plugs, because they don't believe those things are for our day! I do wear the label of being a Full Biblicist.

All Christians are preterists, meaning that they believe in past fulfillments of prophecy, such as Bethlehem (Micah 5:2) and Calvary (Isaiah 53, Psalm 22). I would call myself a "Full Biblicist". I would call those Christians that reject the clear time statements of prophecy, "Shortly" "At

Hand/Near" (Revelation 1:1,3,22:10), and "This generation" (Matthew 24:34), Partial Biblicists. I do NOT partially believe the words of Jeses; I fully believe them! Let me ask my partial Biblicist friends, If Jesus was to come in a kingdom that comes by observation, contrary to Luke 17:20-22, and revamp the physical earth, wouldn't there be a prophecy with a timeline given about such an event? Partial Preterism is truly Partial Futurism. If you leave that door open an inch, the enemy will open it a mile with Futurism. Partial Preterism/Partial Futurism is just a step away from Full Futurism which errors in the same way that the Pharisees did and that modern "Jews" do today. They long for a king in a kingdom that comes by observation (Luke 17:20), and Jesus assures them, "you will NOT see it!"

-Luke 17:22

"The Fall of Jerusalem was, in the fullest sense, the Second Advent of the Son of Man which was primarily contemplated by the earliest voices of prophecy" (Early Days, Vol. 2, p. 489)"

-FW Farrar (1831-1903)

CHAPTER 26

ISRAEOLATRY, NO

BULL!

Matthew 24:32,33

"Now learn the parable from the fig tree: when its branch has already become tender and puts forth its leaves, YOU know that summer is near; so, YOU too, when YOU see all these things, recognize that He is near, right at the door."

First thing here, Jesus is telling His disciples, Peter, James, and John (Mk.13:3) and says, "YOU" three times in this verse, "YOU know…YOU too…when YOU see".

This point alone should annihilate futurism!

Now for what the verse is NOT addressing! Only in the past hundred years have "prophecy experts" interpreted "the fig tree" here to be referring to the modern nation of Israel. If Jesus was meaning to specify the nation of Israel here as being the fig tree, which is actually more commonly referred to as the Olive Tree or the Vineyard, then He would not have said "look at the fig tree

AND ALL OF THE TREES" in the parallel account in Luke 21:29! This verse cancels out such an interpretation. If the fig tree reference was saying, "when Israel becomes a nation again ", then this parallel account would be saying, "when Israel becomes a nation again, and all the nations become nations again". If the fig tree is always referring to the nation of Israel, then what of Jesus cursing the fig tree and executing judgement upon it and saying, "May no one ever eat fruit from you again" (Mark 11:14)? This is what's referred to as an interpretive implosion!

As for this the Old Covenant host nation, it was to be "a light to the nations" (Isaiah 49:6). Israel had bits and pieces of that light, types of Jesus, but once He came to that nation, the light of the world (Matthew 5:14), He fulfilled all of those types! Again, Israel was the type, "out of Egypt have I called my son", and Jesus is the fulfillment and reality of that type (Hosea 11:1), "out of Egypt have I called my Son" (Matthew 2:15) as the Holy Spirit inspired apostle reveals this as he quotes the Old Testament passage in the New Testament. Jesus told the nation that,

Matthew 21:43, *"the kingdom of God will be taken from you and given to a nation bearing the fruits of it."*

What nation was it given to?

1 Peter 2:9, *"You are A HOLY NATION"! Those in Jesus make up this nation of Jews, Gentiles, males, females, bond or free (Galatians 3:28)! They are addressed as "the ISRAEL of God in Galatians 6:16!*

Moses spoke of this same nation , "So I will make them jealous those who are not a people; I will provoke them to anger with A FOOLISH NATION," (Deuteronomy 32:21), which is quoted in Romans 10:19, which was the last days of the Old Covenant people, "what THEIR END SHALL BE" (Deut.32:20), "THEIR LATTER END" (Deut.32:29)!

Isaiah prophesied of this Old Covenant nation being judged and even given "another name", "For the Lord God shall slay you, and call His servants by ANOTHER NAME" (Isaiah 65:15). It's the name of Jesus Christ, where no other name is recognized before God! (Acts 4:12)

Those in Him are called "Christians", according to the Holy Spirit! (Acts 11:26, 1 Peter 4:16)

No people are being "replaced" here, all are being included, as the expansion of Israel has gone global!

Romans 2:28,29, *"For he is not a Jew who is one outwardly, nor is circumcision that which is outward in the flesh; but he is a Jew who is one inwardly; and circumcision is that of the heart, in the Spirit, not in the letter; whose praise is not from men but from God".*

Old Covenant Israel had become "a habitation of demons" (Revelation 18:2)!

They became "the synagogue of Satan"!

Revelation 2:9, *"I know the blasphemy of those who say they are Jews and are not, but are a synagogue of Satan."*

Revelation 3:9 *" those of the synagogue of Satan, who say they are Jews and are not, but lie…"*

ALL things become new in Jesus. The New Covenant, temple, sacrifice, sabbath rest, circumcision, feast days, Jerusalem, and the host nation. All were Old Testament types, fulfilled and realized in Jesus and Jesus alone! That's not good enough for the natural man, he wants Jesus and something more! Jesus and…! The natural man wants a natural kingdom that comes by observation (Luke 17:20-22)! The natural man in the disciples would long for such, but was corrected by Jesus in this passage, "and you shall NOT see it" (Luke 17:22)! Jesus is correcting the natural man in his imagination in our day, void of scriptural revelation, "you shall NOT see it"!

Romans 14:17 *"The kingdom of God IS righteousness, peace and joy in the Holy Spirit", period! The kingdom is not kind of like this, it is exactly as is defined by the Word of God in this verse! Don't add or take away from it, as well as its nature in Luke 17:20,21, "The kingdom of God comes NOT by observation", no ifs ands or buts added here! I like how my friend John Eckhardt puts it, "The kingdom of God comes NOT by observation, see spot run, the kingdom of God comes not by observation "! A relatively well-known radio host once stated, "Yes, the kingdom of God comes not by observation, but it will"! I used to ride public transportation and would interact with fellow passengers on the bus who spoke like this! This confusion is coming from our pulpits! "Now, but not yet", "Jesus is here to come into your heart, heal you, to reveal Himself, but He's coming here soon"!*

Oh, the natural mind that wants to know him according to the flesh (2 Corinthians 5:16)! Scripture says that Jesus was in His flesh for one sole purpose, "a body you have prepared for me"

(Hebrews 10:5), to become a sacrifice! He was in His flesh but has now been glorified to the state He had prior to the incarnation with His father (John 17:4,5) Scripture reveals this speaking of Jesus, "in the days of His flesh" (Hebrews 5:7). This is inferring that He is no longer in His flesh as God the Son, because in the ascension He had to have transitioned from it, "flesh and blood cannot inherit the kingdom of God" (1 Corinthians 15:50). Before the ascension, Martha was corrected as she sought to cling to Jesus before He was glorified (John 20:17). This was just preparing the people for how one ought to get ahold of the glorified Jesus, "though we have known Christ according to the flesh, thus we know Him NO MORE" (2 Corinthians 5:16)!

Jesus had not yet been glorified, even after the resurrection, according to John 20:17. After the ascension though (1 Corinthians 15:50) He was glorified. It was after this that He appeared to John in **Revelation 1:14 as follows,** *"His head and hair were white like wool, as white as snow, and His eyes like a flame of fire;"*

After being glorified in the ascension, He appeared to Paul as "a light from heaven" (Acts 9:3).

So, Jesus is a king in a kingdom that comes NOT by observation (Luke 17:20-22). His kingdom has "nothing to do with some sand in the Middle East", as CL Moore said to redirect my life and understanding of scripture in 1989.

That old covenant host land and nation was used to bring forth the messiah in the New Covenant land and kingdom/nation!

MODERN ISRAEL began in 1948. So, is this a fulfillment of Biblical Prophecy?

"The ideology with the modern Zionist movement has no basis in the Christian reading of scripture, whatsoever…it is idolatry"!

-NT Wright

To start with, it is extremely helpful to understand that Modern Israel is NOT Biblical Israel!

As for the prophecy concerning Israel to be regathered to the land after being exiled from it has a timeline!

Again, timing is everything!

Jeremiah 29:10 "For thus says the Lord: AFTER SEVENTY YEARS are completed at Babylon, I will visit you and perform My good word toward you and cause you to return to this place."

After 70 years in Babylon, they would return to the land, nothing about 2000 years later!

Ezekiel speaks of the same.

Ezekiel 36:24-28 *"For I will take you from among the nations, gather you out of all countries, and bring you into your own land. Then I will sprinkle clean water on you, and you shall be clean; I will cleanse you from all your filthiness and from all your idols. I will give you a new heart and put a new spirit within you; I will take the heart of stone out of your flesh and give you a heart of flesh. I will put My Spirit within you and cause you to walk in My statutes, and you will keep My judgments and do them. Then you shall dwell in the land that I gave to your fathers; you shall be My people, and I will be your God."*

This last sentence is quoted in 2 Corinthians 6:16, but that was really about something 2K years later?

The passage is very simply prophesying of the "new heart", "I will put my Spirit within you", meaning the new covenant, which would come to and through the nation of Israel!

The very next chapter clarifies that this is the New Covenant, "And I will make a COVENANT OF PEACE with them; it will be AN EVERLASTING COVENANT (Hebrews 13:20) with them. And I will place them and multiply them, and set My sanctuary in their midst forever. My dwelling place also will be among them; and I will be their God, and they will be My people." (Ezekiel 37:26,27)

And this last part is quoted in 2 **Corinthians 6:16**, *"And I will be their God, and they will be My people"*. Jeremiah prophesied the same.

Jeremiah 31:31-34 *"Behold, the days are coming, says the Lord, when I will make a new covenant with the house of Israel and with the house of Judah— not according to the covenant that I made with their fathers in the day that I took them by the hand to lead them out of the land of Egypt, My covenant which they broke, though I was a husband to them, says the Lord. But this is the covenant that I will make with the house of Israel after those days, says the Lord: I will put My law in their minds, and write it on their hearts; and I will be their God, and they shall be My people. No more shall every man teach his neighbor, and every man his brother, saying, 'Know the Lord,' for they all shall know Me, from the least of them to the greatest of them, says the Lord. For I will forgive their iniquity, and their sin I will remember no more."*

Again, "I will be their God, and they shall be my people", quoted in 2 Corinthians 6:16.

This entire passage from Jeremiah is quoted in Hebrews 8:8-12, and Hebrews 10:16,17. The Holy Spirit inspired apostles saw this realized in the New Covenant in their day!

In the New Covenant, all things become new, including the capital city and the nation itself. Galatians 4:25,26 speaks of the "Jerusalem above" is what believers are to identify with, not with physical Jerusalem that "now is" (then was), a city representing bondage!

Hebrews reveals this Jerusalem.

Hebrews 12:22 *"But you have come to MOUNT ZION (Is.2:3) and to the city of the living God, the HEAVENLY JERUSALEM, to an innumerable company of angels,"* Notice the flow in Hebrews as the Old Covenant was "ready to vanish away" and Christians were to identify with the New covenant capital city here, "the heavenly Jerusalem" (12:22), so that those things which cannot be shaken may remain" (12:27). Old Covenant Jerusalem would be shaken and would not remain, *"For HERE WE DO NOT HAVE LASTING CITY, but we are seeking the city which is to come"* (13:14)! The New Covenant kingdom would come and be established as the New and True Jerusalem would be seen formally by all as its capital city (Matthew 16:28)!

Remember that the New Covenant Kingdom/Nation was the reality found in the nation of Jesus "Out of Egypt have I called my Son" (Matthew 2:15). This is a quote from Hosea 11:1, which was referring to the Old Covenant type that was the natural nation of Israel. The New Covenant Holy Spirit inspired apostle Matthew sees that the New Covenant fulfills and thereby "replaces" the old types and shadows! Jesus absolutely replaces Israel as the only blessed and safe dwelling place of God! Jesus is the only promised land for any people! It is "another gospel" (Galatians 1:6) that Dispensationalism is offering, "Jesus and....", instead of Jesus alone! It promises a blessing and protection on a people outside of, and even blasphemously against, Christ! Truly a doctrine of demons!

Remember that the kingdom was taken from the Old Covenant nation and given to another nation! **Matthew 21:43** *"Therefore I say to you, the kingdom of God will be taken from you and given to a nation bearing the fruits of it."*

What nation was the kingdom given to?

1 Peter 2:9 *"You are a...HOLY NATION"! This nation is all inclusive, as it breaks down all the race baiters and their attempts to divide into people groups! No people group is left out! This is the nation that was "BORN IN A DAY" (Isaiah 66:8). It's JESUS NATION!*

It really is about Jesus and Jesus alone! Twice in one verse the Holy Spirit makes this point to say that it's not about SEEDS with an "s" at the end, which would mean that it's about many descendants, but it's about the SEED singular, which is Christ and Christ alone!

Galatians 3:16 *"Now to Abraham and his SEED were the promises made. He does not say, "And to SEEDS," as of many, but as of one, "And to your SEED," who is Christ."*

This is a good 3:16 for today's leaders to learn!

The blessing of Abraham is on this SEED alone (Genesis 12:3).

Galatians 3:29 *"And if you are Christ's, then you are Abraham's seed, and heirs according to the promise."*

The Holy Spirit does not acknowledge one's DNA as we see through the words of John The Baptist.

Matthew 3:9 *"and do not think to say to yourselves, 'We have Abraham as our father.' For I say to you that God is able to raise up children to Abraham from these stones."*

The Holy Spirit testifies of the worthlessness and rubbish/dung of Judaism in Paul's life.

Philippians 3:4-8 *"though I also might have confidence in the flesh. If anyone else thinks he may have confidence in the flesh, I more so: circumcised the eighth day, of the stock of Israel, of the tribe of Benjamin, a Hebrew of the Hebrews; concerning the law, a Pharisee; concerning zeal, persecuting the church; concerning the righteousness which is in the law, blameless. But what things were gain to me, these I have counted loss for Christ. Yet indeed I also count all things loss for the excellence of the knowledge of Christ Jesus my Lord, for whom I have suffered the loss of all things, and COUNT THEM AS RUBBISH/DUNG, that I may gain Christ"*

Romans 2:28,29 *"For he is not a Jew who is one outwardly, nor is circumcision that which is outward in the flesh; but he is a Jew who is one inwardly; and circumcision is that of the heart, in the Spirit, not in the letter; whose praise is not from men but from God."*

The Holy Spirit is so spiritual, comparing spiritual things with spiritual things, offending the natural man (1 Corinthians 2:13,14)!

He just turns around and spiritualizes things again to offend modern day Judaizers,

Galatians 6:16 *"And as many as walk according to this rule, peace and mercy be upon them, and upon THE ISRAEL OF GOD."*

Let me tell you, there is NO PEACE outside of the PRINCE OF PEACE and the GOSPEL OF PEACE (Isaiah 9:6, Ephesians 6:15)! It is the "NEW CREATION", in the verse prior, Galatians 6:15, which is the rule of requirement allowing for peace and mercy to be upon a people! Christians are telling a people group today that they are God's people, favored and blessed by Him, all without Jesus Christ! This is absolutely "another gospel" and those spreading it are "to be accursed" (Galatians 1:6,8)!

What about the land promises to Old Testament Israel? I was taught that they never really got all the land and fully possessed it.

Joshua 21:43-45 *"So the Lord gave to Israel ALL THE LAND of which He had sworn to give to their fathers, and THEY TOOK POSSESSION OF IT and dwelt in it. The Lord gave them rest all around, ACCORDING TO ALL HE HAD SWORN to their fathers. And not a man of all their enemies stood against them; the Lord delivered all their enemies into their hand. NOT A WORD FAILED of any good thing which the Lord had spoken to the house of Israel. ALL CAME TO PASS."*

LAND PROMISES FOREVER?

In Genesis 17:7-15 There is an "everlasting covenant" (vs.7) with Abraham. We just went over this in Galatians 3:16,29. What is the "everlasting covenant", if it's not the "everlasting covenant" mentioned in Hebrews 13:20? It's the New Covenant! In it, "the land" is promised as an "everlasting possession" (vs 8) in this covenant. But to be in this "covenant" is the requirement for every man child to be "circumcised" (vs 10)!

Is God requiring physical circumcision of any people today?

The passage says that males "must needs be circumcised. For an everlasting covenant" (vs 13).

New Testament revelation says that "For neither is circumcision anything, nor uncircumcision, but a new creation." (Galatians 6:15, 5:6)! So, for circumcision to be part of an "everlasting covenant", it had to undergo a transition!

Romans 2:28,29 *"For he is not a Jew who is one outwardly, NOR IS CIRCUMCISION THAT WHICH IS OUTWARD IN THE FLESH. But he is a Jew who is one inwardly; and CIRCUMCISION IS OF THE HEART, by the Spirit, not by the letter; and his praise is not from people, but from God."*

Circumcision underwent a transition so as to be everlasting (2 Cor.4:18), so to did the land!

2 Corinthians 1:20 *"FOR ALL THE PROMISES OF GOD FIND THEIR YES IN HIM"*!

All the promises, including THE PROMISED LAND! He's all that and more, but He's not enough for the natural minded man!

Therefore, the land transitioned into Jesus Christ, the only permanent eternal land (2 Corinthians 4:18).

Israel the type (Hosea 11:1), Jesus the reality and only blessed dwelling place of God, This is what is meant when we read,

Amos 9:15 "I will also plant them on their land, And they will not be uprooted again from their land which I have given them, "Says the Lord your God."

Again, just as circumcision transitioned from the visible to the unseen spiritual, so too the land (Genesis 17:7-15). And again,

Galatians 6:15, *16 "For neither is circumcision anything, nor uncircumcision, but a new creation. And all who will follow this rule, peace and mercy be upon them, and upon THE ISRAEL OF GOD"*

One of the ironies in this dispensational doctrines of demons, is those teaching it claim to be for "Jews" today. Yet they believe (wrongly) that 2/3 of those in modern Israel are predestined to be incinerated, according to Zechariah 13:8 "And it shall come to pass in all the land," Says the Lord, "That two-thirds in it shall be cut off and die, But one–third shall be left in it:" So, they are literally paying to have "Jews" flown in from around the world to get incinerated! If any theology is dangerous, or antisemitic, it's definitely dispensationalism! John Hagee actually said, "It's a waste of time to evangelize Jews", contrary to Romans 1:16, 2 Corinthians 6:2, and Matthew 28:18-20). Hagee believes that salvation for Jews is for after the church is raptured. Chuck Smith said the same behind closed doors. I've had pastor friends in high places to tell me so. Dispensationalism is an absolute doctrine of demons!

Dispensationalists believe these truly dangerous things, such as 2/3 of modern-day Jews being predestined to be nuked! Preterists put this number at ZERO! If dispensationalists saw that 2/3 being destroyed as fulfillment in AD 70, this demonic belief system evaporates. What happens when Christian Zionists get off the welcoming committee of such false prophecies and onto the organizing committee, as they are on today in building up the old covenant nation and actively working towards a rebuilt temple and the re-institutionalizing of the sacrificial system? They're literally paying a lot of money towards making this happen!

As for the truth of the Zechariah passage, chapters 12-14 have Jerusalem being judged and Jerusalem being blessed and protected by God. The answer to this dichotomy is found in the previous verses we looked at concerning two Jerusalem's. The one from above, New Covenant Jerusalem is blessed, with the Old Covenant capital city being judged (Galatians 4:25,26). There cannot be peace in Old Covenant Israel, which is absent the Prince of Peace in the gospel of peace (Isaiah 9:6, Eph.6:5), only judgement. Therefore, we must understand which Jerusalem is to be prayed for when scripture says to "Pray for the peace of Jerusalem" (Psalm 122:6). We are to pray for the New and Heavenly Jerusalem, which is from above to invade every city!

Those screeching about "Replacement Theology" are literally replacing the Rock of Christ with modern Jerusalem. Again, all of the Old Testament types, the temple, city and nation are realized in Jesus (2 Corinthians 1:20). We, who are in Him make up the city of the New, heavenly Jerusalem (Matthew 5:14, Hebrews 12:22, "But of Zion it will be said, "This one and that one were born in her" (Psalm 87:5). I think the New Testament says something about being born again"?

Jesus is the Stone of Zachariah!

Zechariah 12:3 *"And in that day will I make Jerusalem a BURDENSOME STONE for all people: all that burden themselves with it shall be cut in pieces, though all the people of the earth be gathered together against it."*

Here's Jesus, The Reality!

Matthew 21:42 *"Jesus said to them, "Have you never read in the Scriptures: 'THE STONE which the builders rejected Has become the CHIEF CORNERSTONE. This was the Lord's doing, And it is marvelous in our eyes'?"*

And Peter expounds on this revelation!

1 Peter 2:6-8 *"Therefore it is also contained in the Scripture, "Behold, I lay in Zion A CHIEF CORNERSTONE, elect, precious, And he who believes on Him will by no means be put to shame." Therefore, to you who believe, He is precious; but to those who are disobedient, "THE STONE which the builders rejected Has become the CHIEF CORNERSTONE ," and "A STONE of stumbling And A ROCK of offense." They stumble, being disobedient to the word, to which they also were appointed."*

Again, Dispensationalism replaces Jesus. Those who are in Him, His covenant people, are the apple of God's eye. There is no longer an Old Covenant, requiring any people to live up to its standards! Therefore, there is no longer an Old Covenant people.

Zechariah 2:8 *"For the Lord of armies says this: "After glory He has sent me against the nations that plunder you, for the one who touches you, touches the apple of His eye".*

Jesus and Jesus alone is the apple of God's eye! A well-known judaizer, Erick Stakelbeck, stated on Lance Wallnau's broadcast, and I quote, "It all comes down to Israel". Replacing, the "all, and in all" of Jesus with modern Israel!

Colossians 3:10 *"Where there is neither Greek nor Jew, circumcision nor uncircumcision, Barbarian, Scythian, bond nor free: but CHRIST IS ALL, and in all."*

Romans 11 is often used by dispensationalists to say that the modern nation of Israel is in the chapter. Yet the dynamics of the chapter are revealed to us when the Holy Spirit says,

Romans 11:5 *"even so, AT THIS PRESENT TIME…"*

The second point to make is that THE CHAPTER MAKES NO MENTION OF THE ACQUISITION OF LAND OR OF MILITARY CONQUEST.

The chapter ONLY SPEAKS OF ISRAEL BEING SAVED (11:26), that such would be life from the dead (11:15).

How is anyone saved! Again, by the gospel and nothing to do whatsoever with acquiring land and military conquest!

Romans 11:26 *"And so all Israel will be SAVED ..."*

"AND SO" is a continuation of thought from the previous verse.

Romans 11:25 *"For I do not desire, brethren, that you should be ignorant of this mystery, lest you should be wise in your own opinion, that blindness in part has happened to Israel until the fullness of the Gentiles has come in."*

"THE FULLNESS OF THE GENTILES" is the harvest at the end of the Old Covenant age (Matthew 13:39). This occurred when the gospel went to the uttermost parts of the earth, which we covered in chapter 13. Matthew 24:14,34 ("Oikoumene" world, Luke 2:1), Acts 17:6, Romans 1:8, 10:18, 16:25,26, Colossians 1:5,6,23 all say this emphatically!

Therefore, when the gospel went out into all the world during those 40 years to the end of the age in AD 70, Jews were saved through this preached gospel! They were gathered into Jesus, though they were geographically scattered throughout the empire (Acts 2:5).

The ESV helps in clarifying Romans 11:26.

Romans 11:26 *"And in this way all Israel will be saved".*

"In this way", referring to the previous verse's mentioning of the gospel going out to the Gentiles. That's how Israel is saved, through the gospel alone!

Note that "ALL Israel" does not mean 100%, any more than God pouring out His Spirit on ALL FLESH meant every man, woman and child on the planet in Acts 2:17. "All" is simply a complete amount. Even futurists believe that only 1/3 of Jews are saved, according to Zechariah 13:8. The word of God literally says that "A REMNANT SHALL BE SAVED" in Romans 9:27.

God had not "cast away His people" as the Holy Spirit says so, in that He had gotten ahold of Paul in Romans 11:1. Elijah is also given as an example of God always saving a remnant in Romans 11:2-4.

Consider God's perspective here.

Romans 9:6 *"For they are not all Israel who are descended from Israel;"*

One of the most scholarly teachers of the Calvary Chapel denomination is John Courson. John stated that the church needs to know of the distinction between Israel and the church. That Israel is the "wife," and the church is the "bride".

Scripture says otherwise without even needing to explain.

Revelation 21:9 *"Come here, I will show you THE BRIDE, THE WIFE of the Lamb".*

They are one in the same, nothing to do with Old Covenant Israel.

God is NOT a two timer!

Those wrongly dividing the word of God will say that the church is a Gentile church and Jews have a separate thing going on with God. The church was started by Jews and the only people in the "church" were Jews in Acts 5:11. It wasn't until Acts 10 when Gentiles were included into the church.

Acts 5:11 *"And great fear came over the whole CHURCH, and over all who heard about these things."*

Many top-named evangelical preachers have said, "Keep your EYES ON ISRAEL". Yet scripture says, "LOOKING UNTO JESUS" (Hebrews 12:2)

I have heard top leaders in the church publicly proclaim that if something happens to Israel, inferring if they were wiped out, then throw away your Bible! Talk about a dangerous belief system! Would they ever consider throwing away their own understanding of the Bible? That they could be wrong about these matters? For many of them, the answer is, no!

The real "Replacement Theology" going on in our day is with dispensational leaders replacing Jesus with modern Israel. I will never forget when Lou Engle did a youth conference at Arrowhead stadium, home of the Kansas City Chief's, and gave an altar call where he pled with the tough and said, verbatim, "Young people, come down and give your hearts to Israel"! I kid you not, these were his exact words calling for the youth to commit idolatry, Israolotry!

As for the simple meaning of the fig tree, it was the season approaching, summer, and would be observable as one would see "all these things, and recognize that He is near, right at the door" (Mt.24:33)

The next verse nukes the idea of any event in the chapter's previous verses being in the distant future!

CHAPTER 27

MATTHEW 24:34

WRONG GENERATION, WRONG DOOR!

Matthew 24:34

"This generation shall not pass, till all these things be fulfilled".

"To write the same things again is no trouble for me, and it is a safeguard for you."

(Philippians 3:1)

Here again, is the definition, usage and revelation of THIS GENERATION in the New Testament.

In Matthew 23:36, we read, *"Truly I say to you, all these things will come upon this generation."*

"THIS GENERATION" can't mean something different here in Matthew 23:36 than what it means in the next chapter, **Matthew 24:34**, *"THIS GENERATION shall not pass, till all these things be fulfilled"*! I had my brother, Dave Warren call Chuck Smith on live radio and he asked him if he thought you could make "THIS GENERATION" in **Matthew 23:36** mean something different in the next chapter in **Matthew 24:34**. He said, "I don't think you can.

Another attempt is made when futurists change "This generation" to "This Race", which no translations do because the Greek word for generation is "Genea", and it is "Genos" that can mean race. Of the nearly 40 times that "Genea" is used in the New Testament, futurist teachers will say that the word always means a generation of people living together at the same time, but the 3 times its used in the Olivet Discourse (Mt.24, Mk.13, Lk.21) it means "race

Let's examine, again, the New Testament usage of "Generation" and how "THIS GENERATION" is used over a dozen times in the New Testament.

Matthew 3:7 *"...O GENERATION of vipers, who hath warned you to flee from the wrath to come?*

Matthew 11:16 *"But whereunto shall I liken THIS GENERATION?*

Matthew 12:41 *"The men of Nineveh shall rise in judgment with THIS GENERATION..."*

Matthew 12:42 *"The queen of the south shall rise in judgment with THIS GENERATION..."*

Matthew 12:45 *"Even so shall it be also unto "THIS WICKED GENERATION."*

Matthew 16:4 *"A WICKED AND ADULTEROUS GENERATION seeketh after a sign..."*

Matthew 23:33 *"Ye serpents, ye GENERATION OF VIPERS..."*

Matthew 23:36 *"All these things shall come upon THIS GENERATION."*

Matthew 24:34 *"THIS GENERATION shall not pass, till all these things be fulfilled."*

Mark 8:12 *"There shall no sign be given unto THIS GENERATION..."*

Mark 8:38 *"...ashamed of me and of my words in THIS ADULTEROUS, AND SINFUL GENERATION..."*

Mark 9:19 *"He answered him, and saith, O FAITHLESS GENERATION..."*

Luke 7:31 *"Whereunto then shall I liken the men of THIS GENERATION?"*

Luke 9:41 *"...O FAITHLESS AND PERVERSE GENERATION."*

Luke 11:30 *"...as Jonas was a sign unto the Ninevites, so shall also the Son of man be to THIS GENERATION."*

Luke 11:31 *"The queen of the south shall rise up in judgment with the men of THIS GENERATION."*

Luke 11:32 *"The men of Nineve shall rise up in the judgment with the men of THIS GENERATION."*

Luke 11:50 *"That the blood of all the prophets, which was shed from the foundation of the world, may be required of THIS GENERATION."*

Luke 11:51 *"...the blood...It shall be required of THIS GENERATION."*

Luke 17:25 *"But first must he suffer many things and be rejected of THIS GENERATION."*

Acts 2:40 *"...Save yourselves from THIS PERVERSE GENERATION."*

Hebrews 3:9,10 *"...forty years. Wherefore, I was grieved with THAT GENERATION." God clarifies here that He is NOT speaking about "THIS" PRESENT GENERATION, by using "THAT" GENERATION within the context of "your fathers".*

"The King left his followers in no doubt as to when these things should happen: "Verily I say unto you, This generation shall not pass till all these things be fulfilled." It was just about the ordinary limit of a generation when the Roman armies compassed Jerusalem, whose measure of iniquity was then full, and overflowed in misery, agony, distress, and bloodshed such as the world never saw before or since. Jesus was a true Prophet; everything that He foretold was literally fulfilled."

-Charles Spurgeon

Dispensationalism says that the majority of God has for you, in His heart, mind, and plan isn't available yet. The authority of the kingdom to reign is not yet. Things have to get worse and worse, darker and darker, with these things taking place all around you, over in the Middle East, then somewhere in the physical sky something will happen, then you can have what God has for you in heaven! Yet, Jesus said that the kingdom is within you and never said a word about you only being able to get only some of it for now! Dispensationalism also teaches, particularly through John

Nelson Darby, that the gifts of the Spirit ceased in the first century. All God has for you is under the Christmas tree, but you can't have those gifts now! Some were for back then, the others are for some day in the sweet by and by!

This is all the doctrines of demons to prevent the power and reign of God from prevailing over evil!

Seeing that the kingdom, righteousness, peace, and joy in the Holy Spirit, is fully established on earth (Matthew 16:28) puts the ball in our court. He is then waiting on us, rather than for us to be waiting on Him to do something. Futurism is looking for something to happen out there, in the sky or in the Middle East, in order for Jesus to take over and reign. I remember hearing Tim Lahaye say that we need to change the words to our Christmas songs, such as "Joy to the World". Those words are, "He rules the world in grace and truth, and makes the nations prove, the glories of His righteousness, and wonders of His love…"

Lahaye says, because Jesus isn't ruling yet.

Scripture says otherwise that Jesus "IS King of kings, and Lord of lords" (1 Timothy 6:15).

Jesus is *"RULER over the kings of the earth"* (Revelation 1:5).

Tim Lahaye asks preterists, where's your hope?

Colossians 1:27 *"Christ IN YOU the HOPE of glory"*!

Our hope is NOT looking for Christ out there somewhere, somehow, someday!

Jesus is the ruler and judge. We don't have to conjure up some fictional worldwide judgement! The following is the judgement coming upon all men.

Hebrew 9:27 *"And as it is appointed for men to die once, but after this judgement,"*

After reading the proofs in this book, which reveal the heart, mind, and plan of God for our future, you have received the renewing of your mind by the truth of His word and been washed from the defilement of a doctrine of demons, dispensationalism (Ephesians 5:26, John 15:3)!

If you have NOT read through the book thoroughly and received it with all readiness of mind and prayerfully searched the scriptures to see if these things are so (Acts 17:11), then please reconsider and do so.

175

It is truly sad to see someone presented with the overwhelming evidence of scripture, which disproves futurism, but refuses to consider something other than what they've been taught!

Often times a person will truly be saddened that the truth of rightly dividing the scriptures on this manner removes an Antichrist, a 7-year tribulation period, an escape from this life, and the incinerating of billions of people. Think about that for a moment. "Don't take away my Antichrist and the nuclear annihilation of billions"! What spirit is this from?

Luke 9:54-56 *"And when His disciples James and John saw this, they said, "Lord, do You want us to command fire to come down from heaven and consume them, just as Elijah did? But He turned and rebuked them, and said, "You do not know what manner of spirit you are of. For the Son of Man did not come to destroy men's lives but to save them." And they went to another village."*

John Hagee offering up strange nuclear fire (Leviticus 10:1)!

Dispensationalism opposes the truth of God's wisdom, therefore, it "loves death" (Proverbs 8:36)! "All those who hate me love death"! Let's reject the dispensational gospel of death and chose life!

John 6:63, *"It is the Spirit who gives life; the flesh profits nothing. The words that I speak to you are spirit, and they are life."*

It is the carnal mind of the Pharisees, set on the flesh, which is death.

Romans 8:6 *"For to be carnally minded is death; but to be spiritually minded is life and peace."*

Dispensationalism's covenant will be judged!

176

Isaiah 28:17,18 *"And your covenant with death shall be disannulled, and your agreement with hell shall not stand; when the overflowing scourge shall pass through, then ye shall be trodden down by it. Judgment also will I lay to the line, and righteousness to the plummet: and the hail shall sweep away the refuge of lies, and the waters shall overflow the hiding place."*

Recommended reading and teaching for the next Reformation.

James Stuart Russel, *"The Parousia". Probably the most scholarly and comprehensive book ever written (nearly 600 pages) on this subject of eschatology, written in 1878.*

Charles Spurgeon said the following concerning "The Parousia", "Though the author's theirs is carried too far (he does not believe this today), it has so much of truth in it, and throws so much new light upon obscure portions of the Scriptures, and is accompanied with so much critical research and close reasoning, that it can be injurious to none and may be profitable to all."

Gary Demar, "Last Days Madness', and any other book written by Gary.

www.AmericanVision.org

David Chilton, "Days of Vengeance", over 700 pages going verse by verse and chapter by chapter through the book of Revelation.

Cyndye Coates, "The Fulfilled Prophecies of Jesus".

Terry Kashian, "The Kingdom Bible".

Don K Preston, All of his multiple books written on this subject.

R.C. Sproul, "The Last Days According to Jesus".

Jonathan Welton, "Raptureless".

Lynn Hiles, "A Study Guide of the Last Days, A Victorious Eschatology".

John Noe, "Shattering the Left Behind Delusion" and "AD 70, The Movie".

Max King, "The Cross and the Parousia of Christ", 800 pages.

Steve Gregg, "Revelation: Four Views, A Parallel Commentary"

Kenneth Gentry, "Before Jerusalem Fell, Dating the Book of Revelation."

C Peter Wagner, "Dominion

Harold R Eberly and Martin Trench, "Victorious Eschatology".

ADDENDUM

GIFTS ARE FOR TODAY!

I believe this, even if someone with the gift of teaching says that such gifts are not for today, as they're teaching cessationism. So, if your teaching gift doesn't exist anymore, is your Bible teaching just your own intellectual ability without the work of the Holy Spirit?

Hebrews 6:5 *"and have tasted the good word of God and the powers of the age to come,"*

If they were only tasting, the appetizer, of the powers of the age to come, then the kingdom age would see more power as the full meal would be partaken of. Is it not "of the INCREASE OF HIS GOVERNMENT and peace there shall be no end" (Isaiah 9:7), which says nothing about a DECREASE?

As I mentioned previously, I liken much of preterist teaching to be the highest and most advanced engine design in the world, only to be accompanied by the belief that spark plugs are not for our day.

A quick repeat for dispensationalists here, the Old Covenant Kingdom/Nation ended when Jesus said it would, with the New Covenant Kingdom/Nation being established as well in the first century (Mt.24:3,34, 16:28, 19:28/Titus 3:5).

It seems that the number one reason cessationists give for the gifts not being for our day is their experience. They went to a church where everyone prayed for healing, for example, and nothing happened, therefore gifts of healing aren't for today.

It is ironic that cessationists say that charismatics base their beliefs based on experience, emotion, etc., and not upon the word. Yet, it is the lack of experience, or bad experience that seems to trump much of the reasoning behind cessationism, not the word alone.

I often hear that if healing is for today then go empty out that hospital. To which I reply, if the gospel is for today then go empty out that mosque!

I have actually prayed for those on their death beds in a hospital and they were healed!

Note that Jesus did not seek out such places but did only those things He saw the father doing in John 5:19.

We see this same thing in **Luke 4:27**, *"And many lepers were in Israel in the time of Elisha the prophet, and none of them was cleansed except Naaman the Syrian."*

1 Peter 2:4 *"who wants all people to be saved and to come to the knowledge of the truth."*

Are all people saved?

And while we're here, the word "saved" (Sozo)involves healing in its definition.

Sozo, to save, i.e. deliver or protect (literally or figuratively):—heal, preserve, save (self), do well, be (make) whole.

Glad that God's not a Gnostic!

We read of this in Isaiah.

Isaiah 53:4 *"However, it was our sicknesses that He Himself bore, And our pains that He carried; Yet we ourselves assumed that He had been afflicted, Struck down by God, and humiliated."*

Christians often teach that this is talking about spiritual sickness and infirmities, yet the New Testament quotes this verse in the context of physical healing.

179

Matthew 8:17 *"This happened so that what was spoken through Isaiah the prophet would be fulfilled: "He Himself took our illnesses and carried away our diseases."*

Again, it is really great to know that God is not a Gnostic, only concerned with spiritual things, but not with issues of our physical bodies.

3 John 1:2 *"Beloved, I wish above all things that thou mayest prosper and be in health, even as thy soul prospereth."*

It is important to remember that the book of Acts records the gifts of the Spirit operating over the time span of thirty something years. It does not, therefore, reveal miracles every other day, but they were dispersed through out this time span.

Let's look at the "cease" chapter where cessationism is derived from.

1 Corinthians 13:8 *"Love never fails; but if there are gifts of prophecy, they will be done away; if there are tongues, they will cease; if there is knowledge, it will be done away."*

First question, is knowledge done away with here? As we will see, it is the "in part" knowledge that is done away with.

To begin with, "cease" means to pause, "Pauo". Jesus ceases (Pauo) to pray in Luke 11:1, where He stopped for a while, yet He would pray after this in a life committed to praying without ceasing (1 Thes.5:17).

Let's consider "Pauo" as stopping or pausing to shift gears. The dynamics of 1 Corinthians 13 have to do with "pauo" occurring when that which is perfect has come, i.e., Jesus in His kingdom.

1 Corinthians 13:10 *"But when that which is perfect has come, then that which is in part will be done away."*

Prior to Jesus coming in His kingdom (Mt.16:28), they saw things "through a glass darkly". After the "pauo" pause, they would see clearly, "face to face".

1 Corinthians 13:12 *"For now we see through a glass, darkly; but then face to face: now I know in part; but then shall I know even as also I am known."*

The same sight issue is seen in **Hebrews 9:8** *"the Holy Spirit indicating this, that the way into the Holiest of All was NOT YET MADE MANIFEST while the first tabernacle was still standing."*

Things were murky and not clearly seen. What would things look like after Jesus establishes His kingdom? Christians were unclear on how much of the law and temple practices they were to be doing in the transition period (40 years) from the Old Covenant age to the coming New Covenant age. After AD 70, it was clear, nothing whatsoever would be required of the Old Covenant system. Their entire Old Covenant old world was leveled with nothing but dirt and ashes remaining! Jesus was the last temple standing. He was "made manifest" as the only temple, capital city and nation in relation to God. I wish dispensationalists would understand this!

So, the gifts operating prior to Jesus coming in His kingdom were operating "in part" as they saw "through a glass darkly". After things became clear, they were to operate "in full", if you will as they saw clearly. The New Covenant temple, Jesus alone, was "made manifest" in Hebrews 9:8.

"In part" pausing for the "in full" clarity is the same as "tasted of the good word of God and the powers" (in part) and "of the age to come" (in full) in Hebrews 6:5. It was the appetizer and the full meal.

The experience of the gifts may have been lacking immediately after AD 70, because of the lack of authentic preachers of the word at the time. Paul said this in Acts 20:29,30.

"For I know this, that after my departing shall grievous wolves enter in among you, not sparing the flock. Also, of your own selves shall men arise, speaking perverse things, to draw away disciples after them."

Of course, no signs of the miraculous (Acts 14:3) would be confirming the word at this time, because it wasn't truly being preached.

This was a definite pause, yet we see throughout church history the gifts at work.

The following is work done on this subject by my partner Terry Kashian taken from The Kingdom Bible (TKB). My commentaries on Matthew, Romans and Revelation can be found in this Bible.

God's Divine Order

The second step in this heavenly culture is God's divine order. Paul says there is an order in the body. He says that firstly, apostles, secondly prophets, thirdly teachers. I first of all want wait say that some today teach there are no longer apostles and prophets. The phrase, "God has placed" is a term that a builder would use when laying a foundation. Paul says in the letter to the Ephesians that apostles and prophets are the foundation of God's living temple that is growing in the Lord. Now I am aware that some say the building of God has already been built and there is no need for apostles and prophets since the foundation has been laid.

Please do not confuse this metaphor with the one Paul uses in this letter stating the Christ is the foundation. This is true, but Paul is making a point in Ephesians about the building of God and Christ being the cornerstone. The Cornerstone joins two walls in one building. Therefore, he was just pointing out in Chapter 2 of Ephesians that Jews and Gentiles are becoming part of one building which the apostles and prophets are the foundation. In every generation God is building and in every generation, He is establishing Divine Order for the time. It is not a prophecy beyond AD 70, but a principle whereby God works to establish in every generation, a testimony of His life and light and love among those who do not know Him. For anyone to say that there are not apostles today would violate two important factors.

One would be that there is not a need for foundational ministry today and more importantly, there is not a need for Divine Order. It is critical to have a foundation in any building and it is crucial to have Divine Order. The church without these two fundamental components is dangerous and is a place where chaos reigns. This could be the contributing factor to our present day situation. Then Paul goes on to say after the three pillar ministries are established in Divine Order in the body. Miracles which is the word 'dunamis' in Greek. We get the word power from this word. It is related to abilities beyond human resources.

I heard one brother say this word could be translated: possibilities. "When His disciples heard it, they were greatly astonished, saying, "who then can be saved?" But Jesus looked at them and said to them, "with men this is impossible, but with God all things are possible." The word for possible is 'dynatos'. Dunamis and dynatos stem from the same root word meaning, to be able, the ability to do. After the three pillar ministries there are those who have a divine ability to do impossible things in people's lives. They are gifted to do the impossible and miraculous and extraordinary.

Then gifts of healings. Possibly we have looked at this backwards through the years. For example, when Peter and John were going to the Temple one day there was a man sitting at the gate begging for alms. Peter saw him and said, "look at us", silver and gold I do not have, but what

I do have I give to you. Rise up in the name of Jesus and walk. Peter pulled him up and his feet were strengthened, and the man went walking and leaping and praising God. Normally, we say Peter certainly had the gift of healing. But I want to propose something that the word gift in 1 Cor. 12:28 is plural and so is the word healing. Peter was giving a gift of healing to the lame man.

The question is who received the gift of healing? Peter or the lame man? I suggest the lame man received the gift of healing. Peter only gave it to him. He was a conduit for the gifts of healings. There should be many in the church that hand out gifts of healings. The next aspect of this Divine Order is helps. Most translate this as assistants, or supports, helps. I looked at this word and found it to be quite interesting. It is made up of two words in the Greek language. One is 'anti' which is instead or against; or as W.E. Vine says, in exchange or in a local sense in front of. The other word is 'lambano' which is lay hold of, to take. So, my sense is that these gifted ones not only help and assist others, but perhaps they take the lead in certain matters and because of their gifting they really help and bless and assist many. Taking the lead is related to this one bringing others into a supply that they do not possess themselves. Then the second to last gifting, we find a word that is normally translated administrations, governing, or governments. The Greek word in this section is only one time in the whole of the New Testament. Kubernesis is the word that we get the English word 'governing'. It is interesting that the Latin origin of this word means to steer. One translation I looked at uses the word 'pilotage'. Not a very common word I would say. When I looked it up I was impressed. Pilotage has one meaning that says, 'the act of piloting an aircraft or ship'.

It is from this definition that we can learn that this gifting is necessary to steer the ship or pilot the aircraft to a specific destination. So, my metaphor of the pilot of the ship or aircraft is obvious, since we are talking about the body of Christ. There are gifted ones in the body that are gifted to steer the church in a specific spiritual direction for the advancement of the kingdom of God. They see practical areas of the purpose of God that can be attained and obtained. Some who are ignorant would say we do not need gifts today and you wonder why some are going in circles or plateaued or have not attained any ground spiritually. Lastly, but let us not minimize the order just as the second from the last is not insignificant. The different kinds of languages. The word for kinds is plural and is the Greek word, 'genos' which is species, race, nationality, family, sort, kinds. In the world there are many languages and in the kingdom of God there are many languages.

Paul says in Chapter 13, if I speak with the tongue of men and of angels indicating that angels do not speak the same language. Speaking in tongues is a stumbling block to many in the church. The question is to speak in tongues or not to speak in tongues? There are different kinds of tongues, and I am talking spiritually now. I will get into more detail as we go into chapter fourteen, but just in passing let me say. Paul shares about speaking in tongues as a means to only speaking to God and not to men. **1 Cor. 14:2-3**. *"... For he that speaks in an unknown tongue speaks not to men, but to God: for no man understands him; however, in the spirit he speaks mysteries."* TKB. Here we see that there is a tongue that is designed for only speaking to God where mysteries are spoken. Paul says, 1 Cor. 14:4, the one who speaks in a tongue builds up himself. Paul also says that when he prays in an unknown tongue, his spirit prays, but his mind is unfruitful. This is not the Holy Spirit praying, but Paul's own spirit that has been born from above.

When a person is born in a certain nation that person is eventually going to speak the language of that nation. When a person is born of the Spirit and from above that person can pray in the language of the spiritual nation that he has been born into unless he is mute. I am not saying that a person who does not pray in a tongue spiritually is not a Christian. I am just saying that he can if he wants to. Then there are anointed tongues that need an interpretation because they are messages to build up, stir up, and cheer up the church. There is a tongue that is for unbelievers also as a sign. Now there are some believers that are unbelievers when it comes to tongues and perhaps God will give them a sign to undo their unbelief. I will cover this more in the fourteenth chapter.

The More Excellent Way

All the parts of the body make up this glorious church which is God's heavenly culture on the earth expressed in diversity and unity with all the multifarious functions. Some go so far as to say there are no apostles or prophets or to the other extreme and say that we are all apostles. We are all prophets. But Paul asks pointedly, "are all apostles"? And again, "are all prophets"? These are rhetorical questions with an obvious conclusion, since he said previously when speaking about the parts of the body. Are all an eye? Are all an ear and where would the smelling be then? It takes the love of God to recognize and respect God's choice in placing the members as He sees fit. It takes faith to trust God and believe He knows what He is doing. I am not talking about self-appointed leaders, but God anointed leaders and gifted ones in the body. The apostle Peter even said, "if any man speaks let him speak as the oracles of God; if any man serves, let him do it as of the ability which God supplies that God in all things may be glorified through Jesus Christ, to Whom be praise and dominion into the New Covenant Age from the Old Covenant Age. Amen. 1 Pet. 4:10-11 TKB. Each one has received the gift of grace to serve one another. There are not ungifted believers. There are only unaware believers of their gift clusters. It takes the body to recognize your giftings. If you are isolated from other believers in a practical way those gifts will not manifest to meet the needs. They are designed to supply the body. The isolated Christian is not able to discover his gifting because what is inside us is manifested when we walk in love. If we are fearful, self- centered, and independent we will not discover our giftings.

These are not designed to exalt individuals. Only the immature get caught in the trap of self-exaltation and superiority over other saints. This is why Paul is emphasizing as we go into Chapter 13 the more excellent way, the way of love. Paul says to desire earnestly the better gifts, the useful gifts. He is not saying that some gifts are more useful or better than others, but he is saying that it is important to desire the gifts that are going to supply the need of the moment in the body. For example, if a person has a disease in his leg and someone prophesies that one day he will run in the fields with his dog and be joyful. This may encourage him as a someday experience. But how much more to desire the gifts of healings and give a gift to the person with the diseased leg so he can run in the fields with his dog. Granted the prophecy may give him hope and another member of the body may get faith when this word is coming forth and give the gift of healing to the person with the diseased leg. This is the body coordinating with each other under the direction of the head, King Jesus. When the more excellent way is followed and walked in, the body builds itself up in love. Eph. 4:16. God's love is the key to having a clear sound and being a clear voice, and truly being something instead of nothing. Ultimately, walking in love is for the profit of all. Everyone benefits from walking this way. The apostle goes on to define what love is and what it is not and when we get to verse eight, he says, "love never falls away". The word for fail is the Greek word, "ekpipto" and two words in Greek, 'ek' is out of or away and pipto, 'fall'. Love never falls out of its place or never falls away. As a star it does not fall out of heaven. As a believer it does not fall away from grace. This word fail is not the same word for when prophecies fail.

Moving From Being a Child or Minor to Maturity

I want to propose something here that may be controversial, but my intention is to discover the truth about verse eight of this thirteenth chapter. It is frustrating to me that so many of my brothers in Christ who testify that they have had experiences of prophesying and speaking tongues but hold to a future fulfillment of the vision of the perpetual purpose of God when it has been fulfilled and all we have to do is walk in it. Then on the other hand I have brothers and not forgetting sisters, who hold that these experiences ended in AD 70 and do not have a demonstration of the Spirit and power of God because it all ended way back when.

I personally speak in a tongue almost daily and have prophesied countless times. I am clear that the truth of something is not based just on experience alone, but I apply the test to myself, not to go beyond what is written. This is the balance and even in the time of our Lord in the days of His flesh there was a problem. There were those who did not know the Scriptures, nor the power of God. We might say that these two camps of believers are among us. Some knowing some of the Scriptures and yet not experiencing the power of God. Then on the other hand there are those who do not seem to know the big picture, but experience God's power which is in faith.

So, we have some believers experiencing these marvels and of course from the camp of believers that believe these ended in AD 70, either say they are of the devil or some psychosomatic experience. They are sure it is not of God because the Lord stopped doing things like this in the 1st century. Then you have people who say, "I spoke in a tongue". I learned it at some charismatic church or ministry. They just told me to say, la la, baba, dada, and I started speaking in some gibberish. They told me I got it, and I was elated because, "I got it"! Some have even spoken in an unknown tongue, but after coming into the knowledge of Full Preterism they have rejected their experience as a counterfeit. First of all, no one ever makes a counterfeit of something that is not real or nonexistent. So that will not fly. But in sincerity we must come to a balanced understanding and my prayer these days is for the Lord to give some understanding, because unless He enlightens, we are all in the dark.

Prophecies and Tongues and Knowledge

As I stated above the word fail connected to love is not the same word in KJV where it uses prophecies fail. This word for fail is 'katargeo'. It is used four times in chapter thirteen.

We will look at each usage. Love never falls away: but whether prophecies, they are put away; whether there be tongues, they will pause; whether there is knowledge, it will be put away. 9 Out of the part we are knowing, and out of the part we are prophesying. 10 But while maturity is coming, then that which is out of the part will be put away. 11 When I was a child, I spoke randomly, I had the mindset of a child, I put things together as a child: but when I had become a man, I put away the immaturity. 12 For the present we are seeing through a mirror, in a riddle; but at that time, face to face: presently I am beginning to know out of the part; but at that time, I will fully know just as I also am fully known. 1 Cor. 13:8- 12 TKB.

Notice that in our TKB translation we omit the phrase 'gift of, connected to prophecies. In the original the word 'gift of' is not there. The word that is normally translated prophecy here is plural. In our translation we keep it plural and omit the gift of. Paul is not referring to the gift of prophecy as we will see. The next time the word 'katargeo' is used, it is in regard to knowledge. This is the Greek word, 'gnosis'. This means to know or knowledge. NT: Strong's #1108. gnosis; gen. gnoses, fem. noun from ginosko (1097), to know. Knowledge. Present and fragmentary knowledge as contrasted with epígnosis (1922), clear and exact [editor's note] Full knowledge which expresses a more thorough participation in the object or knowledge on the part of the knowledgeable subject. The Complete Word Study Dictionary contrasts two words that are commonly translated knowledge in our New Testament. They use the distinction of fragmentary versus full or exact knowledge.

In verse 12, the word epignosis is used and translated fully know and fully known. I like the translation of full knowledge instead of exact. We must consider that the transition saints were under a limited understanding during the transition period between the Old and New Covenant periods. The difference of being a child or minor under the tutoring of the Old Covenant and becoming mature under the New Covenant. Let me bring our full attention to the fact that the things that are being put away are not gifts. Especially not the manifestation gifts that build the saints up. Now there are some that want to include all gifts are put away, but I hope we can see from this presentation that we are dealing with Old Covenant parts and not the powers of the age to come. ... And have tasted the good word (rhema) of God, and the powers of the New Covenant Age about to be coming, ... Heb. 6:5 TKB. If the miraculous has stopped in AD 70, what would Paul be writing about when he states – 'the powers of the age about to be coming'? That age is the New Covenant age which does not end, therefore since we are in the New Covenant age and there is not one after this one, we must still have access to demonstrate the Spirit and power of God.

This is the same power that the saints were to wait for on the day of Pentecost, which was at the beginning of birth of the body of Christ. We have some disconnects when it comes to what continues and what stops in our practice and thinking regarding the Christian life. Today we have some believers still trying to practice Old Covenant things that have stopped, and some believers stop practicing or never start practicing New Covenant things. A little discombobulated don't you think? We should rejoice that we can operate in the spirituals and not depend on our natural or soulish life to build up the saints. This is just wood, hay and stubble! I believe we miss this obvious point in Paul's presentation.

He is always contrasting the Old with the New. Why would he not be doing the same here? In verse nine it says, "out of the part we are knowing and out of the part we are prophesying." What part is Paul referring to? In my study I have discovered that the part is in relation to the progressive revelation of the change God was making in the world. The word part in Greek is meros. This word is used 42 times in the N.T. and translated, part, parts, piece, portion, and coasts and a couple of other words. Paul is saying at the present time we are knowing out of the parts, portions. We just have some of the pieces of the puzzle. Sometimes I think people understand that the apostles had it all together in the first few years of the birth of the church at Pentecost. The Lord was giving it to them piece by piece.

He even gave some of the apostles larger or more pieces than others. For example, when a child is first learning. He is learning by experience not academically. He learns to talk by listening and then repeating what he is hearing. Now do not lose me. The apostles were being taught by listening. Just like a parent would point to a dog and say to the child that is a dog. The child listens and learns. On the day of Pentecost, the Lord poured out His Spirit and Peter stood with the eleven and said, men and brothers, these men are not drunk as you suppose. But this is that which the prophet Joel spoke saying, in the last days God said He would pour out His Spirit. Peter was listening as the Father was pointing to Peter's environment, "this is what Joel was prophesying about". As the apostles were listening they were learning. As time went on they went to the school of the Holy Spirit, where He would lead them and guide them into all reality.

In the early years following the resurrection of Jesus Christ, the apostles found themselves in a unique and transformative period of growth. Much like children learning to read and write, the apostles were beginning to understand, interpret, and articulate the profound truths of the Christian faith. This development did not happen overnight; indeed, it took at least two decades after the cross and many letters during the third decade for the New Testament writings to emerge and complete the canon of Scripture.

In Hebrews 1:1, in the interlinear of the Greek New Testament it starts out, "In many parts and in many ways God of old having spoken to the fathers by the prophets in the end of these days spoke to us in His Son. The word parts or portions is the word in Greek, "polumeros", which is the word in 1 Cor. 13:9, meros, but adding the prefix many to it. Polumeros means many parts. Paul is saying in Corinthians that the saints in the first century were knowing out of the part or out of the pieces. The pieces or parts were the Old Covenant prophets and their prophecies. Prophecies will be put away. Put in a place where they will not be fulfilled again. There is no double fulfillment. There is only the type, which is not perfect and then the reality, the fulfillment.

The next time katargeo is used is with knowledge and this knowledge will be put away. The fragments will be put away because full knowledge replaces the parts. "But as for you, Daniel, conceal these words and seal up the book until the time of the end; many will go back and forth, and knowledge will increase." Daniel 12:4. As Dan. 12:3 says, those who have insight, wisdom and it is not the wisdom of the world, but the wisdom from above and they will shine brightly holding forth the word of life and spreading the knowledge of the Lord over the earth as the waters cover the sea. Leading many to righteousness, peace, and joy in the Holy Spirit. There are two other times the word katargeo is used, but before we go there I want to address the matter of tongues stopping. If we can see that prophecies and in part knowledge or limited knowledge and they pertain to the Old Covenant prophecies and knowledge, then I suggest that the tongue they are speaking about is also related to the Old Covenant.

What Kind of Tongues Are These?

It is interesting that in Daniel there are prophecies, visions, interpretations of dreams all of a prophetic nature. There is also a tongue and an interpretation concerning the judgment of Babylon and Belshazzars' Kingdom. Dan 5:25-29 25 "And this is the inscription that was written:

MENE, MENE, TEKEL, UPHARSIN.

26 This is the interpretation of each word. Mene: God has numbered your kingdom, and finished it,

27 Tekel: You have been weighed in the balances, and found wanting,

28 Peres: Your kingdom has been divided and given to the Medes and Persians."

29 Then Belshazzar gave the command, and they clothed Daniel with purple and put a chain of gold around his neck and made a proclamation concerning him that he should be the third ruler in the kingdom. NKJV

As we mentioned in Dan. 12:4 the prediction about knowledge. The Old Covenant is full of prophecies, tongues, and knowledge in fragments and portions and parts. What kind of tongue will stop? Again, I want to say that this is a proposition and something for the reader to consider. In the Old Testament there are at least three times that I am aware of when the matter of tongues is mentioned. In at least three or four portions of Scripture they all have one thing in common. Tongues were an issue of judgment. The first place is in Genesis 11. The entire land surrounding Shinar experienced a heavy migration, and the people were of one language and their desire was to build something to bring glory to themselves apart from God. They also wanted a place they could retreat into in case God was going to flood them. This is the reason they waterproofed the tower of Babel. Well for the sake of space, we must get to the point. The Lord confused their language by changing their tongues and they could not understand each other and work together. This was God's judgment concerning tongues.

The second and third time tongues is mentioned is in Isaiah 28:11 and Isaiah 33:10. The prediction of tongues is recorded in the middle of judgment on Israel for not listening and obeying and also all the nations. The apostle Paul quotes Isaiah 28:11 in 1 Cor. 14:21 and says, that the tongue is a sign for unbelievers. Isaiah says it is the scoffers, mockers, those who would not listen. Isaiah 28:14-15 says, therefore, hear the word of the Lord, O scoffers who rule this people who are in Jerusalem, because you have said, "we have made a covenant with death, and with Sheol we have made a pact. The overwhelming scourge [punishment] will not reach us when it passes by, for we have made falsehood our refuge and we have concealed ourselves with deception." NASU.

Then the third time is when a tongue is written on the wall. Dan. 5:5, 24, speaks about the writing on the wall in a language that was unknown. In the same hour came forth fingers of a man's hand and wrote over against the candlestick upon the plaster of the wall of the king's palace: and the king saw the part of the hand that wrote. Dan 5:24-25, then was the part of the hand sent from

190

Him; and this writing was written. And this is the writing that was written, MENE, MENE, TEKEL, UPHARSIN.

This was indeed a tongue that only a gifted man could interpret. Daniel operated in the gift of interpreting a tongue, besides dreams, and dark sayings. In this case it was a tongue of judgment. We must see that the uses of tongues recorded in Scripture are significant of the same thing. Babel is a type of Jerusalem; Isaiah 28 is a prediction of the time of Christ when Yahweh judged Jerusalem. Isaiah 28:5- 13, Isaiah admits that what they say is true; because they need to be dealt with in stammering speech and what was unintelligible to them, because of their pride; and the same mode of teaching shall be carried further. "For with stammering lips and another tongue will He (Yahweh) speak to this people." Jamieson, Fausset, and Brown Commentary.

As I mentioned Babylon is the type of Jerusalem according to the Book of Revelation. My proposal is that the tongues that would cease would be regarding the judgment of Jerusalem and the Old Covenant people and system. It is not referring to the prayer language of the New Covenant believer, but the obvious sign to the unbelief of Israel. Even Peter was saved and still needed to see tongues as the Holy Spirit was poured out on Cornelius and his household the same way, Acts 10:44-46 … while Peter was still speaking these words, the Holy Spirit fell upon all those who were listening to the message. All the circumcised believers who came with Peter were amazed, because the gift of the Holy Spirit had been poured out on the Gentiles also. For they were hearing them speaking with tongues and exalting God. NASU.

This was a judgment on Peters' unbelief and later became the testimony to those in Jerusalem. This was a sign to unbelievers. Even believers can act like unbelievers. Acts

11:2-4 … when Peter came up to Jerusalem, those of the circumcision were disputing with him, saying — 'with men uncircumcised you went in, and you ate with them!' And Peter having begun, did expound to them in succession saying …. Acts 11:15-18, as I began to speak, the Holy Spirit fell on them just as on us at the beginning. And I remembered the word of the Lord, how he said, 'John baptized with water, but you will be baptized with the Holy Spirit.' If then God gave the same gift to them as He gave to us when we believed in the Lord Jesus Christ, who was I that I could stand in God's way?" When they heard these things they fell silent. And they glorified God, saying, "then to the Gentiles also God has given repentance that leads to life."

The Generational Model

Theologically Important Statements. In 1 Cor. 13:9, 12 the adverbial ek mérous indicates that our present knowledge and prophesying are only partial. The future age will bring in what is complete. The Little Kittel. I found this little nugget in the Little Kittel that was quite revealing. Even though Kittel was not a full preterist we can see from this little statement some insight into the mindset of the translator. He says ek meros indicates that our present knowledge and prophesying are only partial. Remember that their present age is the 1st century present! This is crucial and the future age will bring in what is complete. These are the two ages. One is the Old Covenant age, and the other is New Covenant age. The full preterist understands the future age, not as outside of time only, in heaven merely, but the New Covenant age that we are in today is perpetual in time and outside of time. This is where I think it gets tricky for us who believe all is fulfilled in A.D. 70.

God's perpetual purpose was coming to a climax and all that was written was being fulfilled and would be completely fulfilled by AD 70. The maturing of God's purpose to bring a full grown corporate man in the fullness of the stature of Christ to full manifestation in one generation was accomplished. It was accomplished in them of the 1st century. Eph. 4:13. I believe this is the generational model for all generations to come, even in our generation. When we become born from above, or born again, we are not full grown. We are newborn babes and need to grow spiritually just as the first century saints did. I hope this is making sense. We are not waiting for the fulfillment of Scriptures that have been predicted, but we are expecting God's faithfulness to all generations including ours.

We are expecting the application of God's fulfilled word in our lives. The application is obvious to me that when we are children, we are going to speak as a child, think as a child, and reason as a child, but when we become full grown we are going to have fuller understanding and knowledge of God's purpose and intention. The difference between the 1st century and us is in the removal of the veil of the physical things of Judaism. We today have our own physical things we need to have removed, but not the Jewish Temple. We may apply the graves clothes of Judaism that try to entangle believers today and get those things removed so we can grow up. For a few years I have been kicking around this matter of a generational model. I haven't heard this used by anyone else, so I am little gun shy to use it. I admit I want the Lord to make me clearer and perhaps those of you who are reading this will be able to build on what is written here.

While Maturity is Coming, Then That Which is Out of the Part Will Be Put Away

Out of the part we are knowing, and out of the part we are prophesying. And while maturity is coming, then that which is out of the part will be put away. When I was a child, I spoke randomly, I had the mindset of a child, I put things together as a child: but when I had become a man, I put away the immaturity. 1 Cor. 13:9- 11 TKB.

Hopefully we are looking at the part in a way that corresponds to the Old Covenant age. It is the age of the minor, the child. As long as the heir remains a child, he does not differ at all from a slave even though he is the owner of everything. This should be an incentive to all who believe to advance and not plateau into what are the grave clothes of Judaism. The external, outward, physical things that we want to make spiritual. It is not the visible things that are infinite but the invisible things. Maturity was the goal of our Lord. His desire of bringing many SONS to glory. Adult sons! We must be clear that this is His desire for every generation. It is about fullness, not fulfillment. It is like a harvest. You start by planting, then applying what is necessary to make it grow. The goal of the farmer is the harvest of a fully mature crop. God is the real farmer! And just as the farmer has a harvest every year so the Lord has a desire for every generation. Some cessationists think the Lord planted in the 1st century and got His harvest in AD 70 and then gave up farming. No, He will be farming perpetually. I hope these things make sense to you.

Remarkably in the Septuagint's translation of the Hebrew text, the same Greek word is used for "riddle" from Numbers 12:8 that is used for "dimly" in I Corinthians 13:12! The idea conveyed is one of imperfection or simply of incompleteness. The precise meaning for the word of the Lord remains enigmatic or a riddle. Prophecy is not always crystal clear. In contrast to others, however, Moses was a prophet who spoke with God "mouth to mouth" and actually viewed the image of the LORD. The Hebrew language is full of idioms which metaphorically refer to parts of the physical body like "mouth to mouth" or "face to face" (see Deut. 34:10). Moses delighted in an intimate and special communication with God which granted him a more indisputable word of prophecy. Significantly, Paul refers to the fact that we peer through the mirror dimly, but at that time "face to face."

The Hebrew idiom, "face to face" is like "mouth to mouth." It definitely seems obvious that Paul is referring to Numbers 12:8. He is referring to Moses and prophecy. The Ancient Rabbis thought that all the other prophets had seen visions and pictured the word of the Lord through a distorted mirror, but Moses beheld visions through a sophisticated mirror as it is said, "he sees the image of Yahweh". Numbers 12:8. The other aspect of the Hebrew idiom of 'face to face', is related to the Day of Atonement. The high priest would enter the holy of holies and inside the holy of holies the walls of the holy of holies were painted with pure gold.

It was in this place that the high priest would see his reflection in the gold. He would see his image in the divine nature of God typified by the gold. This is a revelation of full maturity when we see ourselves in gold. It is substantial that this was on the Day of Atonement. Face to face is also mentioned in Ezekiel 20:35. The context is quite significant since Paul introduced the idea that the children of Israel were a type of the 1st century experience of Paul and those in his day. 1 Cor. 10:11. Ezekiel says that Yahweh was to enter into judgment with Israel face to face. The timing of this is noteworthy, since the time of maturity and the full harvest during the fall feasts were exactly at the time of Israel coming out of the 40-year wilderness. It is at the time of the end of the forty years that Yahweh will cause Israel to face their unbelief, their murder, their resistance to the Holy Spirit.

Ezekiel 20:33-35, As I live, says the Lord Yahweh, surely with a mighty hand, and with an outstretched arm, and with wrath poured out, I will be king over you: and I will bring you out from the peoples, and will gather you out of the countries in which you are scattered, with a mighty hand, and with an outstretched arm, and with wrath poured out; and I will bring you through the wilderness of the peoples, and there will I enter into judgment with you face to face. TKB.

On the one hand Yahweh is going to deliver and on the other hand He will destroy. Just like He did in the wilderness. The first generation that did not believe were destroyed and the second and believing generation, He brought into the Promised Land. The New Testament Promised Land is the realm of the Spirit in FULL MATURITY in Christ as the Promised Land. The Heavenly Land! Paul says, "at that time FACE to FACE we will fully know as we are fully known. What time? The end of the 40 years in the wilderness, the judgment on Old Testament Israel, Jerusalem, the harlot. The time of the harvest or Feast of Tabernacles or the Feast of Ingathering. When did this happen? In AD 70, this was accomplished at the end of the age. We will deal further into the last three feasts in chapter fifteen where the Trumpet and the ministry of Death is put away.

In Chapter 5 we see Christ as the Passover, and then celebrate the Feast of Unleavened Bread as a celebration by cleaning out the old and making way for the new continuously. Getting rid of the Old Covenant practices and worldly practices and making way for the New Covenant practices. Leaving the elementary principles concerning the Christ and pressing on to maturity.

This seeing through a mirror is quite interesting as I pondered on this. Whenever a person looks into a mirror that person sees himself. Consider what the Lord is implying. Paul starts out by saying we are seeing through a mirror in a riddle. Perhaps beholding the Lord is becoming clearer in what He is like in us. As we mature we are seeing Him in us as our character because He is transforming us into the same image, from Old Covenant glory to New Covenant glory. 2 Cor. 3:18. 1 Peter 1:7-8 … even though tested by fire, may be found to result in praise and glory and honor at the revelation of Jesus Christ; and though you have not seen Him, you love Him, and though you do not see Him now, but believe in Him …. 1 John 3:2-3 Beloved, now we are children of God, and it has not appeared as yet what we will be. We know that when He appears, we will be like Him, because we will see Him just as He is. This is crucial when John is saying we are children. Not adults, but children. The Greek word is teknon instead of huios. The difference is between, not mature and mature. This word "teknon" is different from Paul's phrase, 'when I was a child'. Paul's use of child is even younger than John's usage. This is just a thought where Paul's usage is approximately 5-7 years earlier than John's. This could be the difference between the maturity levels in the Greek word, nepios in Corinthians and teknon in 1 John. There is so much more to say on this matter.

Paul closes this chapter with three things that remain or abide. Faith, hope and love and the greater is love. Some think that when we pass on we will not need faith because we will live by sight. Every description of those who tell us what heaven is like or the afterlife speak in terms of sight. Yet Paul says that faith remains. Hope or expectation remains. Love is infinite! God is infinite and He is unsearchable and unfathomable. In infinity we will still operate in faith, hope and love. While we are here we must pursue love because nothing is greater than love. Love never falls away, never fails, and is the crowning jewel of the Christian life. The word for greater in this verse is also translated in Romans 9:12 when comparing Esau and Jacob. It is NT: Strong's 3187 meizen and is translated older. We may get from this that this is a sign of maturity when we are loving with God's love.

II. Interpretation of the Greek word "Pausontai"

In 1 Cor. 13:8 normally translated cease there are alternative definitions to the word that is used.

Greek Word: παύω

Transliteration: pauō

Phonetic Pronunciation: pow'-o

Root: a root verb ("pause")

Cross Reference:

Part of Speech: V3 historical contexts. For instance, during periods of persecution or spiritual opposition, the manifestation of spiritual gifts may decrease, indicating a temporary pause in their expression (Wagner, 2002). Further support for the interpretation of "Pausontai" as a temporary cessation comes from Hobart Freeman's study on spiritual gifts. Freeman suggests that this pause serves the purpose of facilitating spiritual growth, character development, and the maturing of believers. Thus, spiritual gifts not only benefit individuals but also contribute to the edification of the body of Christ (Freeman, 1994).

B. Examining the relation of "Pausontai" to the concept of spiritual gifts in the early church

In the early church, the interpretation of "Pausontai" played a significant role in shaping the understanding of spiritual gifts and their manifestation. The concept of a temporary pause or cessation of these gifts offers a delicate perspective on the experiences and practices of the early believers. Jeff Doles' research highlights that the early church recognized the ebb and flow of spiritual gifts, which were manifested through the ministry of the Holy Spirit. This recognition conveyed an understanding that the expression of spiritual gifts was not constant or uniform, but rather influenced by various factors, including the spiritual climate and the needs of the church (Doles, 2006). W.E. Vine's contributions to the interpretation of "Pausontai" emphasize the role of divine sovereignty in the utilization of spiritual gifts. Vine suggests that the temporary pause signifies the Holy Spirit's control over the distribution and manifestation of these gifts. This perspective underscores the importance of spiritual discernment and reliance on the leading of the Holy Spirit when exercising spiritual gifts (Vine, 1991).

C. Discussing the implications and significance of this interpretation

The interpretation of "Pausontai" has profound implications for understanding the dynamism and fluidity of spiritual gifts in the early church. Recognizing the temporary nature of the pause in the expression of these gifts allows for a more nuanced understanding of their manifestation and highlights the importance of discernment within the body of believers. Furthermore, the interpretation of "Pausontai" raises questions about the relationship between spiritual gifts and the broader work of the Holy Spirit in the life of the church. Charles Sullivan's research emphasizes that the pause in the manifestation of spiritual gifts should not be seen as a withdrawal of the Holy Spirit or a diminishment of His power, but rather as a strategic pause to facilitate spiritual growth and maturation. This understanding challenges the notion of spiritual gifts 4 as solely sensational or miraculous, encouraging a more balanced view of their purpose and function (Sullivan, 2002).

1. Crisco, C. Greek (2010).

2. Wagner, C. Peter - Pausontai: The Temporary Cessation of Spiritual Gifts in the Early Church (2002).

3. Freeman, H. The Manifestation of Divine Power Through Spiritual Gifts (1994).

4. Sullivan, C. The Dynamic of Spiritual Gifts in the Early Church (2002).

5. Doles, J. E. Flowing in the Supernatural Power of the Holy Spirit (2006).

6. Vine, W. E. The Ministry and Gifts of the Holy Spirit (1991).